MARY
Icon of the Spirit and of the Church

FRANÇOIS-XAVIER DURRWELL

MARY

ICON OF THE SPIRIT
AND OF THE CHURCH

Translated by Robert Nowell

 St Paul Publications

Original title: *Marie: méditation devant l'Icône*
© Editions Médiaspaul 1990

Cover painting by Salvatore Fiume

St Paul Publications
Middlegreen, Slough SL3 6BT, United Kingdom

Copyright © St Paul Publications 1991

Printed by The Guernsey Press Co., Guernsey, C.I.

ISBN 085439 364 1

St Paul Publications is an activity of the priests and brothers
of the Society of St Paul who proclaim the Gospel through
the media of social communication

Contents

Preface

What I am offering is a meditation. I would like to present to people's eyes an image, the image of a woman mentioned only once by St Paul and then anonymously as just 'a woman'. But she is evoked in the Trinitarian setting of the Father who sends and of the Son and the Spirit who are sent: 'But when the time had fully come, God sent forth his Son, born of woman... God has sent the Spirit of his Son into our hearts' (Gal 4:4,16). Mary is the handmaiden of low estate (Lk 1:48) and is only that; but God has used her for the service of his own mystery, that of begetting the Son in the power of the Spirit, when it pleased him to make this mystery a reality in this world.

* * *

Despite numerous requests, I hesitated for a long time. It was not because of lack of interest in the one of whom Jesus said: 'Behold, your mother!' It was because my theological method has always been to take passages of scripture as the basis for my reflections – and scripture seems so niggardly on the subject of Mary. In addition I have preferred to reflect on those aspects of the Christian mystery which theology has left more or less in the dark – and so many books tell us about Mary. What could I add?

True, the passages of scripture are few and far between, but they are rich, capable of nourishing a prolonged meditation. As far as originality is concerned, broadly speaking this remains possible, despite everything: the paschal mystery, from which here too as in all my other works I draw my inspiration, is the inexhaustible source of an illumination that is always new. The image of Mary starts to shine with an unwonted brilliance once it is exposed to the light of Christ's passover.

My lengthy hesitation was thus not due to the embarrassment that many people feel when faced with the praise that the Church incessantly lavishes on Mary. They find it too much. They ask if Mary is not being raised above the common condition of humanity. Sometimes they send us back to the oldest of the four gospels, that of Mark, which presents Mary so simply as the same as other women of her race: a good Jewish mother.

Let us not forget that Jesus too was of low estate: '[He] emptied himself, taking the form of a servant, being born in the likeness of men' (Phil 2:7). If everything had ended for him on the cross, one could believe that history would not even have remembered his name. But 'God has highly exalted him and bestowed on him the name which is above every name' (Phil 2:9). When in Jesus the disciples recognized Christ the Lord (cf Acts 2:36), they were not slow to become aware of the glory that dwelt in this humble Jewish mother. From then on they gained the assurance that 'all generations will call [her] blessed' (Lk 1:48).

If, as the poet wanted to say, one is allowed to compare small things to great, one could reflect on what happened to an obscure young Christian woman of our age, Sister Teresa of the Child Jesus: 'I am a tiny seed,' she said one day as reported in her *Last conversations*, 'and one does not yet know what it will give rise to.' What it gave rise to was, in the words of Pope Pius XI, like a 'hurricane of glory'.

A saying that applies to every Christian is: 'Your life is hid with Christ in God' (Col 3:3). It is of everyone that it is said: 'It does not yet appear what we shall be' (1 Jn 3:2). Every believer carries within himself or herself a 'weight of glory beyond all comparison' (2 Cor 4:17). Mary carried within herself 'the Lord of glory' himself (1 Cor 2:8).

The glory of Mary, like that of those who believe, is only perceived by faith. It is the job of theology to 'look not to the things that are seen but to the things that are unseen; for the things that are seen are transient, but the things that are unseen are eternal' (2 Cor 4:18).

One of the most legitimate desires is to want not to remove Mary from the common condition of humanity. To meet this there are two possibilities. One consists of failing to take account of her peculiar and individual grace, to let her image become blurred and indistinct so that it melts back into the anonymity of the crowd. One might as well keep silent about her and about this insignificant presence which would not kindle any hope in the world. But one can also recognize her grace and proclaim Mary as 'blessed... among women' (Lk 1:42). It is the very peculiarity and individuality of her grace that place her 'among all women', at the very core of humanity. These qualities make of Mary our neighbour, the closest there can be next to Christ.

The peculiarity and individuality that belong to Mary are those of fullness and not those of exception. God grants her, in its fullness, the grace bestowed on the whole Church, offered to the whole of humanity. She is the icon of the salvation which God brings about for us in Jesus Christ. In contemplating this image Christians have the joy of discovering the grace that God intends for them.

Part 1

ICON OF THE SPIRIT

1

In the shadow
of the Spirit

In Nazareth a girl got engaged. The very year when she was going to be taken into Joseph's house she was ravished in 'the glory of God': 'The Holy Spirit will come upon you, and the power of the Most High will overshadow you' (Lk 1:35). God himself had prepared her wedding finery and, without taking her away from Joseph, indeed in giving her to him (Mt 1:20), he brought her to his own dwelling where he is the Father of the only Son.

Nobody except her fiancé, when he learned this unexpected news, imagined the radiance that surrounded this girl. They had to wait until the mystery of the child was revealed so that the mother would appear on high in the heavens clothed in the light that the Bible calls 'the glory of God'.

'And a great portent appeared in heaven, a woman clothed with the sun, with the moon under her feet, and on her head a crown of twelve stars' (Rev 12:1). She was pregnant and, because she was pregnant, clothed with the sun.

'The glory of God' is a mysterious reality. It is the 'flashing radiance of the divine being',[1] the indication of God's sovereign presence, the manifestation of his power: 'In the morning you shall see the glory of the Lord' (Ex 16:7), 'Did I not tell you that if you would believe you would see the glory of God?' (Jn 11:40; cf Jn 2:11). It is said to be like a cloud with at one and the same time the brightness of light and the density of darkness. This cloud guided the people of the Exodus, covered the top of Mount Sinai, filled the tabernacle of God in the desert and the Temple on the day it was dedicated. According to Isaiah (4:5) it will be spread over the assembly gathered on Mount Zion when the days that have been foretold come. It overshadowed Jesus and his three disciples when he was transfigured (Mk 9:7).

The angel said to Mary: 'The power of the Most High will overshadow you' (Lk 1:35). The thick cloud of light that is called the glory of God will overshadow you, will clothe you in light: a woman surrounded by the glory of God.

The New Testament has given this glory a name that at first sight seems not to be related to it, since the phrase Holy Spirit means not glory but the breath of God. Nevertheless Isaiah (63:10-14) had already seen in the pillar of cloud by day and the pillar of fire by night that guided the people of Israel on their

14

exodus an image of the Holy Spirit. The first epistle of Peter (4:14) talks of 'the spirit of glory and of God'. 'The Holy Spirit' – which is the glory of God – 'will come upon you' and will enfold you in its bright shadow.

The Holy Spirit for its part is God's power being made manifest. The two terms 'spirit' and 'power' are inseparably united throughout the Bible and are found linked with 'glory': together, the Spirit and the Power and the Glory bring about God's mighty works. This is why the three together provide the unique cause of Jesus' resurrection: he 'was raised from the dead by the glory of the Father' (Rom 6:4), 'lives by the power of God' (2 Cor 13:4), was raised in Christ: at one and the same time in the glory and in the power, and they will be raised 'a spiritual body', that is to say, transformed in the Holy Spirit (1 Cor 15:42-44). Under the three names one and the same cause is at work, the Holy Spirit of God.

At Nazareth 'the spirit of glory and of power, the spirit of God'[2] laid hold of an Israelite girl and made of her the mother of God's Son in the world: 'therefore the child to be born of you will be called holy, the Son of God' (Lk 1:35). The child will be Son of God because he will be born under the all-powerful action of the Spirit. How are we to understand this link between the Holy Spirit and the divine sonship of the child?

God is Father. His glory, his power is in his fatherhood, in the infinite begetting of the infinite Son. This is how his inmost mystery was made manifest when God revealed himself 'in these last days' (Heb 1:2), in the burning bush of the ultimate revelation which is Jesus in his passover: he is 'the God and Father of our Lord Jesus Christ' (2 Cor 1:3).

The New Testament keeps the term 'God' for him whom theology calls the first person of the Trinity: 'There is one God, the Father,... and one Lord, Jesus Christ' (1 Cor 8:6). The entire mystery of this God the Father is to be found in his infinite fatherhood with regard to the infinite Son. His person is formed in this begetting: his eternal and all-powerful activity is exhausted in the infinite begetting of the infinite Son. It is in this way that God reveals himself in Christ: when he raises Jesus from the dead and brings it about that 'in him the whole fullness of deity dwells bodily' (Col 2:9), the mystery of God is revealed as that of a God the Father, as God going out of himself into an infinite Son. This, as Paul is reported as preaching (Acts 13:33), is how the saying is fulfilled: 'Thou art my Son, today I have begotten thee' (Ps 2:7). After Jesus' resurrection, the disciples know that 'God [is the] Father of our Lord Jesus Christ' (2 Cor 1:3; 1 Pet 1:3).

Now it is in the Holy Spirit that God raises up his Son. He raises him up by the power (2

Cor 13:4); he raises him up by the glory (Rom 6:4); he raises him up by the Spirit (Rom 8:11). The Spirit is the all-powerful working, the active person by whom the Father accomplishes his works, by whom he produces his first and in some way unique achievement: the begetting of the Son. The Spirit is the glory that puts the Father in ecstasy outside himself. It is the love (Rom 5:5) in whose fertility is born the Father's 'beloved Son' (cf Col 1:13). It is thus the depth where the mystery of the Father who begets and the Son who is begotten is accomplished, the vital force of begetting: it is the mysterious womb of the Son's conception.

They are three: the Father, the Son and the Holy Spirit. 'They are three: the one who loves, who is loved, and love.'[3] They are three: the begetter, the begotten, and the divine begetting.

A modern saint has gone as far as to say: 'The Father begets, the Son is begotten, the Spirit is the process of conception; it is their personal life by which they are distinguished from each other. The Spirit is thus this conception, very holy, infinitely holy, immaculate',[4] by which God is the Father, the Son is the Son.

I have just said it, but it needs to be said again, since this excellent truth is so little known: the Spirit fulfils its role of divine begetting conspicuously at the point where the mystery of God is fully accomplished in this world, in Jesus' passover. At this culmination of his human existence Christ attains the fullness of his own birth as Son. 'What God promised to the fathers, this he has fulfilled to us their children by raising Jesus; as also it is written in the second psalm, "Thou art my Son, today I have begotten thee"' (Acts 13:32-33); the Son was 'designated Son of God in power according to the Spirit of holiness by his resurrection from the dead' (Rom 1:4). It is in the power, it is in the glory, it is in the Spirit who is the divine begetting that God has raised him up. Ever since, the Church has known with certainty that God is the Father, that Jesus is his only Son, and theology is able to conclude that the Spirit is the divine begetting or, to put it in the feminine, is the divine conception, the Spirit who is the power in which the Father raises up his Christ.

Every believer is caught up in the Spirit of the Father who raises Jesus up: he or she is 'raised with him' (Col 2:12); with him, he or she is begotten by the Father in the Holy Spirit (cf Gal 3:26, 4:4-6). He or she is born from on high, 'of water and the Spirit' (Tit 3:5). In primitive thought water is a feminine and maternal symbol; in Christianity it is raised up to the dignity of the sacrament of 'birth from on high'. Now the Bible sees in water – that of springs and fountains and that

18

of rain – the symbol of the Spirit of God being poured out: 'I will sprinkle clean water upon you, … I will put my spirit within you' (Ezek 36:25,27); 'For I will pour water on the thirsty land, and streams on the dry ground; I will pour my Spirit upon your descendants' (Is 44:3; cf Is 32:15, Zech 12:10, Jn 7:37-39). The children of God are born from Baptism as from a mother's womb. From the water they are born of the Spirit of which water – with its maternal connotations – is the symbol.

This maternal role was played by the Holy Spirit first of all in the earthly birth of the Son of God: the Spirit played this role jointly with a woman. Jesus is the man who is Son of God, born at one and the same time of the Spirit of God and of the womb of Mary: 'The Holy Spirit will come upon you, and the power of the Most High will overshadow you; *therefore* the child to be born will be called holy, the Son of God' (Lk 1:35). The Son's earthly conception is brought about in a synergy[5] of heaven and earth, in the collaboration of the All Highest who is the Holy Spirit[6] and an earthly being: not the Spirit and an impersonal reality such as the water of Baptism, but the Spirit of the All Highest and the womb of a woman of the earth.

In Jesus' family tree as recorded by Matthew the verb 'beget' is kept for the men and the role of the women is expressed by the preposition 'of': 'Judas begat Phares and Zara of Thamar; ... and Salmon begat Booz of Rachab; and Booz begat Obed of Ruth; ... and David the king begat Solomon of her that had been the wife of Urias' (Mt 1:3,5-6, AV).

Talking of the birth of Jesus, the evangelist uses the same preposition 'of' three times: once when speaking of Mary 'of whom Jesus was born' (Mt 1:16), and twice when speaking of the Holy Spirit: 'she was found to be with child of the Holy Spirit' (1:18), 'that which is conceived in her is of the Holy Spirit' (1:20).[7]

It belongs to the Father to beget the Son in the world. His role is evoked by these words: 'That which is conceived in her is of the Holy Spirit' (Mt 1:20). By whom was it conceived? In biblical language, God's action is often expressed by a verb in the passive: this rhetorical device allows one to indicate God without using his name.[8] It is God who begets this child in Mary and does so in the power of the Spirit.

Sometimes people like to call Mary 'the spouse of the Holy Spirit'. But nothing in either of the two gospel accounts – that of Matthew and that of Luke – suggest any analogy between the role of the Spirit and that of a husband. Conceived of the Spirit and of Mary, Jesus is 'Son of God', not of the Spirit of God (Lk 1:35). God is the Father who begets and the Spirit is his action: it is the glory which puts God in ecstasy outside himself in his Son; it is the power of the

Father in his fatherhood; it is the divine fecundity, the holy, infinitely holy, immaculate conception. 'The Holy Spirit will come upon you', it will envelop the girl in its all-powerful glory, it will take her into itself and make of her on earth what it is itself in God. Mary is the human understudy of the Holy Spirit. She is the womb where God's work in his eternal fatherhood is accomplished on earth. Jesus is born divinely and humanly of his God and Father, conceived at one and the same time in the Holy Spirit and in a young Jewish girl. Mary's motherhood is the transposition on to the human scale of the Holy Spirit in its eternal action.

The mystery of the Trinity thus enters into the world and is realized there. In Jesus, God is the Father at the heart of the world: he begets his Son at one and the same time in his own womb which is the Spirit and in a creature taken up in this Spirit. He had chosen the Jewish nation and, like a husband, was bound to it by love. 'Rejoice,' the angel told Mary, 'it is on you that God's favour has come to rest' (cf Lk 1:28). God's love for the whole of Israel has become concentrated on this single girl and draws her into the orbit of the eternal mystery. A great sign appeared in heaven, a woman clothed with the sun, in whom God accomplished in the world the begetting of his Son.

The Holy Spirit does not bear a name that

allows us to form a picture of it. We know what a father is, what a son is. But the Spirit of God is without a face. Its name, whether in Hebrew or Greek or Latin, means breath and it is also called fire, living water, the power of God, love – all impersonal names. Nevertheless, 'the Spirit of the Lord has filled the world' (Wis 1:7), but its presence is invisible. In the same way in human history mothers often remain without a name: in the Bible they are hardly mentioned in the family trees, even though it is they who maintain the fabric of humanity. Their work is inward. Nevertheless there was in history a moment when God gave his Spirit a face: in a woman whom he took up into the mystery of his Spirit. More than any other creature she is marked with the 'seal of the Spirit' (cf Eph 1:13, 4:30): more actually than the water of baptism, which is virginal and maternal, she is the symbol of the eternal conception, the holy icon of the Spirit of God.

By the thrice-holy Spirit of God Mary is holy Mary, she in whom there has been expressed in the world the mystery of God's holiness, that of the conception of the Son.

* * *

Mary was the symbol of the Spirit of divine conception at the first moment of her motherhood: she did not cease to be so, either during the nine months of her pregnancy, or when the child was born, or during the long period of dependence which is a child's education. In the eternal today of his father-hood the Father does not cease to feed the Son at the bosom of the Spirit which is infinite divine love, power and holiness;[9] on earth the Son was fed at the bosom of Mary. The role played by the Holy Spirit in the education of every child of God was a role the Holy Spirit played first of all with regard to Jesus and did so through Mary. The Spirit teaches us to pray (Rom 8:15,26; Gal 4:6): Mary taught her child to pray, suggesting to him the gestures he should make, the phrases he should utter. The law required parents to teach their children the *Shema, Yisrael*: 'Hear, O Israel: the Lord our God is one Lord; and you shall love the Lord your God with all your heart, and with all your soul, and with all your might. And these words which I command you this day shall be upon your heart; and you shall teach them diligently to your children' (Deut 6:4-7). The mother whispered into her child's ear, and the Spirit awoke his heart, bringing to his lips that invocation filled with a child's trust: 'Abba!' Mary must have been surprised at this. Never had she heard anyone address the Lord God with the loving familiarity of a small child addressing his father.[10] Because the Holy Spirit overshadowed her, in all her work as a mother, Mary's teaching bore unexpected fruit: the child's prayer went beyond what his mother taught him, just as by the work of the Spirit the child born of Mary was more than just the son of a woman.

It is in this way that the Spirit and the mother continued to work together in the work of the incarnation. The Word was made flesh in Mary by the power of the Spirit, while at the same time the Father's eternal praise that is the eternal Word became a human invocation: 'Abba! Father!' 'Christ Jesus, high priest of the new and eternal covenant, taking human nature, introduced into this earthly exile that hymn which is sung throughout all ages in the halls of heaven' (Vatican II, *Sacrosanctum Concilium* §83), the hymn to the glory of the Father. In the beginning was the Prayer, and the Prayer was made man.

Mary is greatly exalted – 'He who is mighty has done great things for me' (Lk 1:49) – and God is so humble. The Father is God in the infinite begetting of the Son and he grants to a daughter of men to share in what his divine greatness does. Mary could say to God when talking of Jesus: 'Our Son – yours and mine.' Even more admirable than Mary in her exaltation is God in his humility, introducing a creature into his glory.

* * *

God has a single Son whom he begets in the omnipotence of the Spirit. But he wishes to embrace men and women in this unique begetting: he raises them up with Christ (Col 2:12), he takes hold of them in the power of *his* resurrection (Phil 3:10), which is the Spirit of divine begetting and thus makes of Christ the first-born among many brethren (Rom 8:29).

Mary remained for ever marked by the seal of the Spirit which is the power of divine begetting. The mother of Jesus, she became also the mother of those who believe, but in a different way.

The Fourth Gospel likes to omit Mary's name so as only to recognize this woman in her role of mother: 'The mother of Jesus was there' (Jn 2:1); 'But standing by the cross of Jesus were his mother and his mother's sister' (Jn 19:25). Jesus adopts an unusual and generic mode of address for her: 'Woman, what have you to do with me?' (Jn 2:4); 'Woman, behold your son!' (Jn 19:26). At the moment when the history of salvation swings over and moves from the flesh to the Spirit, when Jesus becomes 'a life-giving spirit' (1 Cor 15:45), Mary no longer has to give life according to the flesh. But nevertheless she remains mother: 'Behold, your mother!' Jesus tells the beloved disciple (Jn 19:27). The seal of motherhood that the Spirit imprints on her is indelible.

This is Mary's identity for ever. *Theotokos* is her name. She is devoted to the mystery that belongs to the Spirit, to the service of the holy conception of the Son in the world.

* * *

It happens that Mary makes herself visible in a domain that is hers, in the Church which too is mother by the grace of the Holy Spirit. One day, this Church, through the mouth of the parish priest of Lourdes, asked her to disclose her name. The beautiful lady that appeared devoted herself to prayer for weeks. To give her name she waited for the day from which she drew her name, the day of the holy conception. On the morning of the feast of the Annunciation, 25 March 1858, she reappeared, 'small and young' as when she was betrothed and did not delay replying. She opened her hands that had been joined together, lowered her arms, then raised them, resplendent with gratitude: 'I am the Immaculate Conception.' Bernadette went to the parish priest and told him: 'She answered: "I am the Immaculate Conception."'

Mary does not call herself merely immaculate in her conception, exempt from the stain of original sin. Of course she affirms this, but she indicates infinitely more. Her unique and unshareable grace, her eternal identity, the name that characterizes her is not to be found in being exempt from the sin of Adam. God could have protected other creatures from their beginnings from the evil which has from the start spread over the world (Rom 5:12).[12] Moreover, every Christian is freed from original sin by Baptism which raises him or her up, beyond the sinner Adam, to the point of the divine sonship of Christ who 'is before all things' (Col 1:17). There is a grace more radical than that of being born exempt from 'the stain of the sin of Adam.'[13] Again, no human being is radically a sinner, as God does not create sinners. At root man is created in Christ and directed towards Christ (Col 1:15-16): sin only ever comes about on top of this, seeking to contradict the covenant of fatherhood and sonship which by creating God has established between himself and his creatures. At root man is immersed not in sin but in an original grace because, before being dependent on a first man, he is created by God in his Christ and for his Christ.[14]

Mary bears a unique name. What the Holy Spirit is, the holy divine conception, she is in human terms: she has been taken up into the function of the Holy Spirit. This is her grace, this is her name.

Lourdes is a symbol. Everything there makes one think of, everything suggests, the name of the woman who appeared. Mary let herself be seen in a grotto. In primitive thought a cave has meaning: it is where the earth, where everything has its birth, opens up. Christian fancy was no doubt inspired by this primitive symbol to place Jesus' birth in the grotto of Bethlehem when St Luke merely records that the child was placed in a manger (Lk 2:7).[15] More, water is everywhere at Lourdes, that of the Gave and that of the spring, water which is a feminine and maternal symbol from which Christianity creates the sacrament of being born from above. In this symbolic framework Mary reveals the name which she has received from God and which she shares as a human being with the Holy Spirit.

'Blessed are you among women', was how Elizabeth greeted her (Lk 1:42), the most blessed of all.[16] In the Bible a woman's glory is in motherhood. Elizabeth recognizes in Mary the most wonderful motherhood there could be.

2

Since the dawn of creation

The angel Gabriel was sent by God to a girl in a town of Galilee called Nazareth (Lk 1:26). In the Bible an angel is a messenger from God: he is God's face and voice, the manifestation of his will. Since the dawn of time the angel has been on his way towards this meeting with this girl. Indeed, the woman crowned with stars (Rev 12:1) has been pregnant since the garden of Eden in Genesis. The Messianic seed is placed in her with the saying: 'I will put enmity between you and the woman, and between your seed and her seed; he shall bruise your head' (Gen 3:15). Standing before the woman is the dragon, 'that ancient serpent', ready from the start to swallow up her child (Rev 12:4,9; cf Rev 20:2). Eve, the mother of all the living, is the first name of the Messianic woman, but Mary is her definitive name. Through the distant ancestress and the long generations is seen she who among all women is the mother of the child who 'shall bruise your head'.[17]

The Father's plan was engraved in the

world even before the history of the first men, since everything is created in Christ and for him and everything subsists in him (Col 1:15-17). The seed of the final creation has already been sown in the first. God is the Father, the essential Father; all his activity is to be found in the begetting of the only Son; he only acts, he only creates in the act in which he is God, in that of his fatherhood with regard to the Son: 'all things were created through him and for him.' The earth has always been destined to bear in itself the Son and the Host of his brethren reunited in him: 'All things were created through him and towards him' (Col 1:16).[18]

The Father begets the Son in the Spirit. It is necessary to repeat this: the Spirit is the power of God in his fatherhood, the womb where the Father begets the only Son and in which his other works come to be born. It is thus in the Spirit that the Father brings about his filial creation, and the earth is born under this fluttering of maternal wings: 'And the Spirit of God was moving over the face of the waters' (Gen 1:2). The creation is thus filial, created by the Father in the begetting of the Son; but it is also maternal, created in the Spirit which is like God's womb and which from the earth makes the womb from which human beings are born. Job (1:21) affirmed: 'Naked I came from my mother's womb.' As this is like a miniature form of the universal

30

womb which is the earth, he was able to add: 'And naked shall I return.'

The Holy Spirit which is God's transcendent holiness and the physical matter that seems to be its diametric opposite meet each other. Between the Spirit in its pure spirituality and creation in its materialness there reigns a surprising closeness.[19] Creation is material and maternal but it is also spiritual, thanks to the Spirit which is the womb of God; just as Isaac, though a child according to the flesh, is said to have been 'born according to the Spirit' (Gal 4:29). The Spirit, the creator, the eternal divine conception, lets the earth be maternal, be the womb in which God will beget his Son in the world, the cradle of him for whom everything has been created (Col 1:16). It was brooding over the primordial waters, over these virgin and maternal waters; one day it would brood over a woman. Nothing is as close to the earth as woman,[20] and each woman is marked by the seal of the Spirit in whom God conceives his Son. Is it not this consecration which allows the writer of 1 Timothy to say: 'Yet woman will be saved through bearing children' (1 Tim 2:15)?

Sown throughout the whole of creation, the Messianic promise was subsequently focused on a privileged nation and was accomplished in a girl of this nation. The Spirit which brooded over the waters and encompassed this nation overshadowed Mary and brought to maturity in her the fruit that had always been promised. This woman's vocation goes back to the dawn of creation: it is that of the earth, that of Israel, brought to full term. The liturgy takes this as its authority in placing these words in her mouth: 'Ages ago I was set up, at the first, before the beginning of the earth' (Prov 8:23).[21]

In Mary the whole earth is honoured. In her every woman is honoured in her motherhood. And in her and for ever Israel, the maternal nation, is honoured.

3

The woman without sin

At the creation of earth and mankind from which the incarnate Son would be born their countenance was not tarnished by sin. Mary, from whom the Son would be born, shared the original innocence which, in her, was all the more dazzling as the earth, and mankind would see the fruit of their motherhood come to maturity in her womb.

The Church believes that Mary was 'conceived without sin'. The phrase uttered at Lourdes says more than this, but also says and confirms this. Mary precedes the world's first sin and every other sin: she is 'younger than sin, younger than the race from which she has sprung'. Born millennia after the first sinner, she is prior to him, much younger than he: she is 'the youngest daughter of the human race', 'our little youngest sister',[22] she who never reached the age of sin.

Jesus, to begin with, precedes our common ancestor, even if he is called 'the last Adam' (1 Cor 15:45). He is a descendant, but his origin is in the eternal begetting where he is born of the Father in the holiness of the Spirit: 'He is before all things' (Col 1:17). Mary is created in this mystery of the Son, inseparable from him in her original innocence, prior in her motherhood to the sin of her ancestor.

When the annunciation came to surprise her, grace had already prepared her for this grace: 'Rejoice, you who are full of grace.' To translate it properly one should add this nuance: 'You whom grace has made holy, you who have been made pleasing to God.'[23] Right from the beginning she was sanctified with a view to this annunciation. The motherhood of the woman crowned with stars of which Revelation speaks dates from the origins of mankind. 'That ancient serpent', the one mentioned in Genesis, has always been there before the woman ready to devour the child at his birth (Rev 12:4). There have always been enmities between the pregnant woman and the serpent because of the Messianic seed she is bearing. The saying of Genesis 3:15 applies to Eve, the distant ancestress, because of the Messiah who was to be born, and applies even more to her in whom the Messianic motherhood comes to term.

A stone that falls into a deep pool of water spreads ripples across the whole surface. In the same way the Son who enters into the world spreads his grace outwards from the point of his entry into time. It goes back to the origin of Mary's life and to the beginning of the world, in Eve whom God takes back into his favour: it continues until the end of Mary's life and until the conclusion of the history of the world, in order to lead to glory both Mary and the world. The world – and Mary first of all – is created with Christ as its starting point and as its goal. In all things Christ is the alpha and omega (Rev 22:13).

Thus for Mary the innocence of her entry into existence flows from her relationship of motherhood to him whose begetting in the world is the source of all grace. The mystery of the pregnant woman (Rev 12:1), of whom it is said from the beginning: 'I will put enmity between you and the woman' (Gen 3:15), is in the first place the mystery of Mary.

* * *

The common theological explanation used to be that it is in anticipation of the merits of Christ that Mary from her conception was preserved from the stain of original sin that has marked the whole human race. This kind of language affirms a certain truth but is open to criticism.

It involves thinking of God as a creditor who lets a debtor off a debt because he foresees that one day someone else will pay it. But God is essentially the Father: his role is not to anticipate and reckon up his Son's merits but to beget him. Scripture does not represent the mystery of salvation on the model of an accounts department where Christ pays a price on behalf of men and women and God subsequently 'applies' to them the merits acquired on their behalf.[24] God saves men and women as Father, by begetting his Son for them in the world. He begets for them through the life and death of Jesus, up to that fullness of begetting which is the resurrection (cf Acts 13:33). He who is essentially the Father of the Son saves us in Jesus Christ by becoming *for us* the Father of this unique Son.

As for Jesus, he is essentially the Son and it is in this role that he saves us, in filial consent to his Father who begets him for us. Through life and death the Father leads him for us to his fullness as the Son, in his resurrection when the Father proclaims: 'Today I have begotten thee' (Acts 13:33 quoting Ps 2:7). Jesus lets himself be consecrated (cf Jn 10:36) by his Father who begets him, up to the ultimate consecration in his death and resurrection (Jn 17:19). In his death that leads to glory, not only does he acquire merits for us but he becomes redemption for us (1 Cor 1:30). Jesus is the salvation of the world in person: in him are saved those who enter into communion with him. The Father, whose role is not to reckon up and distribute merits but to beget, begets the Son for us and encompasses in the begetting everyone who is in communion with Christ.

Mary has been made holy right from her beginnings not simply by virtue of Christ's anticipated merits but through communion with him. The mystery of God who begets the Son in the world is spread over the world, is spread first of all over Mary whom God makes sharer in this begetting. Her original innocence comes from this sharing, from this close proximity.

Close to Christ, Mary is close too to men and women, by virtue of the holiness without stain which nevertheless distinguishes her from them. Christ himself who is completely holy is above all the one who shares in solidarity with sinners, since holiness – which is communion – does not separate.

Furthermore, everything is not evil in sinful humanity: Mary is not an isolated island of white purity in a tide of universal blackness. The sin which has overrun mankind since its beginnings has not corrupted it to its roots. Otherwise how could Christ who is all-holy share in solidarity with it? Between him and mankind there reigns a relationship of kindred, through God who creates man in and for Christ (Col 1:15-17): God creates the world at the core of the mystery of his fatherhood with regard to Christ and the programme for

Christ. At root man is thus not immersed in sin but is the work of God's favour, of the Father's love with regard to the Son. What is primary is the relationship to the Creator and to Christ and this is more profound than solidarity with our ancestor who sinned. God does not create sinners: the sin which from the start weighs on the world (Rom 5:12) is something that came after. It can obstruct the call to communion with Christ; but even though obstructed the call survives. Chapter 3 of Genesis, which tells of the sin of Adam, does not obliterate the earlier pages which speak of man created in the image of God.[26] It is this radical holiness, fragile, overlaid by sin, which allows the Holy One of God (cf Mk 1:24) to enter into solidarity with the sinful world. Christ came to save and bring together the scattered children of God (cf Jn 11:52).26

Mary belongs to sinful humanity by the very grace that distinguishes her from it. Her original holiness does not separate her: it is a privilege not of exception but of completion. Mary's beginning coincides with the original universal innocence in which humanity was created; but, in her, innocence is brought to the summit of its potentiality to the point that sin has not been able to survive. With the whole of mankind Mary has been created in Christ and for Christ, but in her the relationship with Christ is of such immediacy that sin has not been able to squeeze in between her and her Saviour.

Here we find a first application of a principle proper to Mary's privileges: the abundance of her grace does not separate her from, but places her at the inmost core of the Church and mankind.

The history of theology proves that the truths of faith can find their expression in different languages that are more or less close to their truth. The theology of the immaculate conception provides an illustration of this.

(a) When Mary's immaculate conception was proclaimed a truth of the faith in 1854 there had predominated for centuries a theology of original sin according to which every man and woman is born a sinner, under the domination of sin, beyond any grace and by this fact is excluded from the order of salvation. The privilege of the immaculate conception would on this view have been a pure exception, isolating Mary from the rest of mankind.

(b) Moreover, the theology of redemption was largely derived from a juridical mentality: Christ had paid God the price needed to meet the demands of God's justice and to reconcile him with men and women. In anticipation of these merits of Christ, God preserved Mary from the stain of original sin, applying these merits to her in advance.

(c) This juridical kind of theology went on to assume a break between the work of creation and the work of redemption, a double plan of creation and of salvation. For a humanity created to begin with in innocence and with no need of being saved in Christ was substituted a sinful humanity on whose behalf God introduced a new plan, that of redemption. Mary belonged to this second humanity. If God had not preserved her from the stain of original sin by anticipating the merits of Christ she would have entered into existence as a sinner.

In our days theology has become more aware of the scriptural data and has freed itself from a juridical cast of mind. It recognizes in general the unity of the work of creation and that of redemption. From the start of history every man and woman is, in the core of their being, created towards Christ, looking towards the salvation which is in Christ (cf Col 1:15-17). In her immaculate conception Mary belongs to mankind created in innocence and destined for Christ. Thanks to her immediate closeness to Christ, in whom and towards whom all things are created (Col 1:15-17), she is the creature made holy whom the sin of mankind cannot touch. She is and remains prior to original sin (c).

Her original grace, her immaculate conception, thus does not separate her from the rest of mankind, every man and woman having been created in Christ and towards Christ. It is a privilege of fullness and not of separation: it roots Mary into the heart of the human community (a). It is above all an outstanding grace of sanctification and not in the first place the absence of a stain (a).

Finally, Mary is made holy not only in anticipation of Christ's future merits but because of her immediate relationship to Christ, the source of grace, for whom and towards whom all things are created (b).

4

The virginal and maternal creature

The Spirit which is divine conception brooded over creation and made it maternal, able to bear children and ordered towards the birth of the Son – for 'all things were created towards him.' The earth was born virgin and already at the same time maternal, maternal in its virginity, through the power of the Spirit.

This original moment of creation, of virginity and motherhood at one and the same time, comes out into history in Mary and finds its fulfilment in her, by the same power of the Spirit. The time of completion when God sends his Son born of a woman corresponds to the primordial time and brings the latter to its perfection. The final realities have been prepared in secret from the start: 'I will utter what has been hidden since the foundation of the world' (Mt 13:35 quoting Ps 78:2).

Mary's virginity is a question neither of deprivation nor of sterility. Under the shadow of the Spirit of divine conception, Mary is just as much mother as virgin. The girl from Nazareth has not just remained a virgin: she has become the blessed virgin, the woman whose virginity is in this motherhood. The Spirit of divine conception is the source and the seal of her virginity.

Mary is not isolated by this privilege: she is not separated from other mothers, among whom she is blessed more than all the rest. This is because she is not the only one to have been marked by the seal of the Spirit, even though no other is her equal in her virginal motherhood. Of course, no other woman becomes pregnant except by a man: nevertheless in the conception of every child there is an element where God's creative fatherhood is direct. In what is most human in man, in what he is in his inmost being, his conception is virginal: as a person he (or she) is not the product of the biological laws that preside at his birth. He is a person, a child of God, who comes from God who creates him as such, by reference to the communion with him and with men and women in Jesus Christ. This reference is 'spiritual': it comes from the Spirit, the creator, the cause of all personalization.[27] Under this aspect, every birth of a human being is virginal: in every mother a heavenly spark comes down to earth to catch fire.[28]

If it happens that a birth is marked more than another by God's intervention and by relationship with Christ – such as the birth of Isaac – St Paul does not hesitate to declare that it comes from the Spirit (Gal 4:29). In the woman who is blessed among all others God's paternal action is powerfully asserted. Mary is the mother of a child who, in his person, is God's own Son, towards whom every human person has been created and whom God will claim entirely for himself when he says over him while raising him up in the Holy Spirit: 'Thou art my Son, today I have begotten thee' (Acts 13:33 quoting Ps 2:7). In Mary's virginal motherhood we find the expression in human terms of the mystery of God who begets the Son in the Holy Spirit.

Woman's double beauty thus shines out in Mary, that of the girl in the bloom of her youth and that of the mother. In her, the fruit ripens without the flower fading: indeed, it is the fruit that gives the flower its brilliance. In her is honoured the virginal and maternal earth over which the Holy Spirit broods; in her is honoured every woman who brings into the world a child of God and the 'daughter of Zion', the Messianic nation which, through the Spirit, bore the Messiah in its womb. In her God the Father is glorified who knows no other Father than God. And in her is glorified the Spirit which reveals itself as the mysterious womb, as the holy conception, by which there is in God a Father and a Son.

5

Holy Mary

We turn to her saying: 'Holy Mary, mother of God, pray for us.' She is 'holy Mary' because she is the mother of Jesus Christ.

In the Bible holiness is not in the first place a quality of the moral order, a perfect assemblage of virtues. God is holy by the fact of his transcendence, by the infinity of his mystery: man is holy by consecration to God. That is why St Paul could call the Christians of Corinth saints, even though many of them were not without their faults.

God's holiness is being the Father who begets the infinite Son in the omnipotence of love which is the Holy Spirit: it resides in his infinite fatherhood. The Spirit is God's holiness in person, because it is the power of begetting, the divine conception, by which one is the Father and the other is the Son.

Mary for her part had the grace to share in the begetting of the Son in this world. God's holiness took her under its shadow and consecrated her. Mary is holy in this maternal consecration, she is 'the immaculate conception'. Anyone who fully acknowledges the mystery of the incarnation is induced to venerate 'holy Mary, mother of God'. Sharing in the holy conception of the Son is something that happened only to her, to her uniquely.

But before admiring this creature one can be amazed at the infinite love which God displays to her, just as to the whole earth which in Mary has borne this fruit: 'God so loved the world that he gave his only Son' (Jn 3:16). From this St John drew the conclusion: 'God is love' (1 Jn 4:8,16). Not only does he give his Son: he shares with the earth, and with a woman of the earth, the mystery of the divine begetting in which he is God.

Those who take offence at the devotion with which the Church surrounds the mother of Jesus sometimes raise the objection that to bring a child into the world does not make anyone holy, since 'the flesh is of no avail' (Jn 6:63). Does not Jesus reply to the woman who praises his mother: 'Blessed rather are those who hear the word of God and keep it!' (Lk 11:28)? But in speaking in this way Jesus is asking this woman to raise herself above earthly realities: he is not finding fault with his mother whom Elizabeth, inspired by the Spirit (Lk 1:14), congratulated on her faith in the word and her obedience (Lk 1:45). In taking her under its shadow, the Spirit also impregnated the heart of the 'handmaid of the Lord'.

I hope the reader will forgive the language I am about to use. Modern surrogate mothers are asked to lend their wombs but are forbidden to be true mothers, to develop personal relationships with their children. Those who will not allow Mary to be involved in her heart in the mystery of the incarnation, to be personally consecrated in this mystery, want God to have turned her into the world's first surrogate mother. No: she is the true and holy mother of the Son of God.

'Rightly therefore the holy Fathers see her [Mary] as used by God not merely in a passive way, but as co-operating in the work of human salvation through free faith and obedience' (Vatican II, *Lumen Gentium* §56).

There are 'extrinsicist' theologies in which the mystery of the incarnation is never accepted in the realism of its depth. In this case Mary is not recognized in all truth as *Theotokos*, as mother of a God-man; the Church is not truly regarded as the body of Christ, in communion with Christ in the work of salvation; the believer does not see himself or herself as radically justified but simply overlaid by God's justice. Fundamentally, in this case one dare not believe that in Jesus Christ God became totally involved in mankind.[29]

Today, as at the time of Nestorius, to recognize in Mary the holy *Theotokos* is a criterion of belief in the realism of the incarnation.

6
The heart of Mary

According to one tradition the evangelist Luke was a painter. He is supposed to have captured Mary's looks in a painting which the makers of icons were subsequently at pains to reproduce. It is a legend. But Luke in fact offers us a very fine portrait of Mary which has not ceased to inspire artists.

He speaks of the 'heart' of this young woman who was about to become a mother: 'But Mary kept all these things, pondering them in her heart' (Lk 2:19). A little later he uses the phrase again: 'His mother kept all these things in her heart' (Lk 2:15). In the language of the Bible 'the heart' is the inmost depths of a person where communion is established with God, where the intelligence and the will find they are undivided and from where thoughts and feelings arise, where free decisions are worked out.

Mary for her part speaks of her 'soul [which] magnifies the Lord' (Lk 1:46). The word means at one and the same time the being in its depths and the entire person.[30] It is in this way that the psalmist sighs: 'My soul waits for the Lord more than watchmen for the morning' (Ps 130:6).

How can one sound the depths of Mary's heart? How can one explore her soul? In the depths of herself Mary is the mother of Jesus. She is this by the gift of God and in her acceptance of this gift: 'Let it be to me according to your word' (Lk 1:38). In the depths of herself Mary welcomes God who, in her, begets his Son in the world.

The annunciation is told in the style of a drama being played between God and his creature. The curtain rises, God is present through the ministry of the angel. The gift is offered, the creature is invited to welcome it. There follows the moment of the crisis when the drama reaches its moment of tension, when the solution remains in suspense but is being sought in a moment of reflection, questioning and explanation. At last the crisis is resolved and Mary agrees. The angel leaves her, the curtain falls, the mystery of God who begets his Son in the Holy Spirit becomes reality in the world.

The essential thing about Mary's soul is proclaimed when she says: 'Let it be to me according to your word.' Elizabeth congratulates her: 'Blessed is she who believed' (Lk 1:45). What is specific to faith is to welcome the gift of God: 'His own people received him not. But to all who received him, who believed in his name, he gave power to become children of God' (Jn 1:11-12). Mary's role, her merit, was to believe, to welcome: 'The angel announces, the virgin hears, believes and conceives. Faith in the mind, Christ in the womb.'[31] The primal creation over which the Spirit broods, all-embracing, pregnant with the gift of God, reaches in Mary the fullness of time (Gal 4:4): its motherhood reaches its term.

When people receiving communion open their hands and their mouths and their hearts they are performing the act typical of faith. In her soul and in her body Mary welcomes him who is the Word: she is the model of faith.

Welcoming faith is itself a gift of God, a fruit of the Spirit. St Paul is definite on this point: 'No one can say "Jesus is Lord" except by the Holy Spirit' (1 Cor 12:3). The person who believes is said to be 'full of faith and of the Holy Spirit' (Acts 6:5, 11:24). Mary believes and agrees in the power by which she conceives: by the Spirit which overshadows her, by the grace of her virginal motherhood, just like the Church of which Vatican II has said: 'By the power of the Holy Spirit, she preserves with virginal purity an integral faith' (*Lumen Gentium* §64).

Faith and maternal virginity go hand-in-hand in Mary. Her faith is itself virginal: it depends on God alone, looks for salvation in him and believes in the impossible. The girl

Mary surrenders herself to 'the power [that] is made perfect in weakness' (cf 2 Cor 12:9), to the God of the impossible (Lk 1:37) who 'is able from these stones to raise up children to Abraham' (cf Mt 3:9). In her believing virginity Mary is a wonderful symbol of faith. The Spirit is the power of her faith and of her motherhood and the seal of her virginity: it calls forth life in Mary by giving her the faith which welcomes this life. Faith forms part of the grace of motherhood which God grants Mary.

While being completely receptive Mary is not passive: she co-operates in her heart and in her body. The Spirit which has taken possession of her is the dynamism of God: it spreads in men and women by making them share in its activity. By receiving faith is active: it welcomes with eagerness. The saying of the Fathers and of earlier theologians that Mary conceived in her soul before conceiving in her body[32] corresponds to God's mode of action: his grace is given in making itself welcomed by faith.

Mary's *'fiat'* was thus not a statement of resignation but of longing and gladness: 'Let it be to me according to your word' (Lk 1:38). The Messianic rejoicing to which the daughter of Zion was often invited by the prophets (Zech 2:10, 9:9) breaks into the girl's heart. 'Rejoice', says the messenger and joy bursts forth, the joy of the Holy Spirit which is the joy of God in his fatherhood with regard to the Son. Mary becomes a mother, by the gift of God, and of such a child! A powerful feeling as yet unknown springs up and breaks forth: 'My soul magnifies the Lord and my spirit rejoices in God my Saviour, for he has regarded the low estate of his handmaiden' (Lk 1:46-48). God has looked upon her and Mary has woken, as the earth reveals itself in the morning when the glance of the sun rests on it.

To know this heart one would need to be able to plumb the mystery of the Spirit in which Mary was taken up in her motherhood.

The Spirit has been described as God's humility. It exists in fact completely in relation to others: to the Father of whom it is the Spirit of fatherhood, to the Son of whom it is the Spirit of sonship. It never asserts itself in face of the other: It is his inwardness and depth. It is neither the Begetter nor the Begotten; it is neither the Lover nor the Beloved, neither the Revealer nor the Revealed; it is the Begetting, the Love, the Revelation, all at the service of the Father and of the Son. Mary, invaded by this mystery, lives in relation to the Father by whom she is a mother, to Christ whose mother she is: her heart is of crystal, a pure transparency. Like the Spirit which, in God, is the operative person, the divine operation by which he is the Father, the love in which he begets, Mary is 'the lowly handmaiden of the Lord', the mother of the Son. Just as the Spirit does not have a name – the term 'breath' by which it is known is not really a person's name – so Mary, at least in the gospel according to St John, does not have a name: she hides herself behind her role and is called 'woman', 'the mother of Jesus' (Jn 2:1-4, 19:25-27).

But humility does not humble people. The Spirit that is the humility of God is also his glory and bears the name 'Spirit of glory' (1 Pet 4:14). In him God's immense greatness breaks out, his power of infinite fatherhood, of unlimited love. Humility is the welcome that Mary gives to the power of God. In her destitution she lets herself be clothed with the sun.

7

The loving mother

At the core of her being Mary, that pure transparency, is also goodness and tenderness. Her heart is maternal, at one and the same time crystal and loving.

This is because the Spirit who is relationship is the relationship of love: 'God's love has been poured into our hearts through the Holy Spirit which has been given to us' (Rom 5:5). God begets the Son in this mysterious and fathomless womb which is the Spirit and he begets him by loving. In this love the one is the Father, the other the Son, begotten in love, 'his beloved Son' (Col 1:13).

Note that the Spirit of love, the divine begetting because it is infinite love, takes hold of a girl; that the Father begets the Son in the world jointly by means of the Spirit who is love and through a girl taken up into this Spirit.

The power to love which penetrated Mary's heart had to be pure and broad and deep. It was the eternal mystery of love with which she was linked, this unique begetting of love which, through her, was realized in the world too. To beget Jesus, his Son in the world, God does not repeat the eternal act of his fatherhood of love. He is only a father once; but the power of eternal begetting, this infinite act of love which is the Spirit of the Father, translates itself in human terms into Mary, the icon of the Spirit. The Son who as God is born in love is born in love also as man.

Beyond this, it is for the love of men and women that the Father begets the Son in the world: 'God so loved the world that he gave his only Son' (Jn 3:16). Faced with God who gives his Son, that is to say who begets him for us in the world, John wrote: 'God is love' (1 Jn 4:8). In Jesus, God is the Father for us, the Son is begotten for us, the Spirit is the divine begetting for us. Mary is brought into the mystery of an unfathomable love where God exists for us.

'I will ... give you a heart of flesh. And I will put my spirit within you.' In the first covenant the Spirit is made manifest as power; but in this prophecy of Ezekiel (36:26-27) the way is prepared for the revelation of the Spirit who is love. The heart of stone, which cannot be reached by the word of God or the cry of the poor, has been changed. There where the Spirit penetrates he creates a heart of flesh. Elizabeth cries out: 'Blessed are you among women' (Lk 1:42). To this woman with the greatest fullness of motherhood the

Spirit has surely given a heart that is motherly beyond compare.

All the same, allusions to this love are rare in the gospels. There is mention of a sword that will pierce Mary's soul (Lk 2:35). There is the record of that saying laden with sorrow: 'Son, why have you treated us so? Behold, your father and I have been looking for you anxiously' (Lk 2:48). Without a doubt it was she who suffered the most, but it is Joseph's suffering she is concerned about first: 'Your father and I.' Perhaps she was persuaded by the family to make the approach that Jesus found hardly welcome when he was told: 'Your mother and your brothers are outside, asking for you' (Mk 3:32). But had she not been persuaded above all by her heart which wanted to see her son again? Then the hour came when the sword wounded the whole of her and threatened to destroy her life. Then love expanded to match the immensity of sorrow. Mary became able to welcome the saying: 'Behold, your son!' (Jn 19:26).

Ever since, without exhausting them, the Church has drawn on the treasures of pity and tenderness in this heart. On earth, Mary was a humble woman, apparently a simple Jewish mother. In reaction against what is judged to be an excessive Marian piety it happens that this simplicity is emphasized so as to conclude that Mary remains what she was on earth: a simple Jewish mother. But this is totally to ignore the eschatological mystery of the resurrection when what was weakness, the humble earthly reality, bursts into life all of a sudden through the power and glory of the Spirit (cf 1 Cor 15:43-45).

On earth, no human heart is infinite to the point of embracing within itself all men and women. Every Christian's life is hidden (Col 3:3), confined within narrow limits: what it will be has not yet been made clear (1 Jn 3:2). Jesus himself was a being full of weakness, his activity was limited to a tiny region, to only one nation (Mt 10:5-6, 15:24), 'being born in the likeness of men' (Phil 2:7). But when the alabaster jar was broken to let its precious perfume escape, the whole house was filled with the fragrance of the ointment (cf Jn 12:3). In his death that glorified him Christ 'fills all things' (Eph 4:10); those who believe 'will appear with him in glory' (Col 3:4); and the love of Jesus' mother is spread maternally through the entire earth.

Nobody has been taken up as she has into the maternal role of the Spirit, has been endowed with such a grace of charity. She is the human reflection of the Holy Spirit who is in person the mercy of the 'Father of mercies' (2 Cor 1:3), the infinite love in which the Father begets. The Church knows this by experience: Mary's maternal love has become universal and no argument can count against this experience.

8
A thoughtful heart that struggles

What she accepted in faith Mary kept in her heart: 'But Mary kept all these things, pondering them in her heart' (Lk 2:19). She turned them over in her mind, compared them with each other, organized and co-ordinated them. Right at the moment of the annunciation she 'considered in her mind what sort of greeting this might be' (Lk 1:29). When Jesus asked his parents: 'Did you not know that I must be in my Father's house?' the evangelists record the same questioning incomprehension: 'They did not understand the saying which he spoke to them...; and his mother kept all these things in her heart' (Lk 2:49-51). What had happened was so mysterious that she had to spend her time tirelessly searching out its meaning and by plumbing its depths her own heart was made more profound. She went on living wrapped in that Spirit of whom it is said: 'The Spirit searches everything, even the depths of God' (1 Cor 2:10).

She knew, but without really understanding: what she heard and what she experienced were enough to bring about the obedience of the handmaiden of low estate. If the splendour of the mystery had been made manifest to her, would she have been able to bear the weight of everyday life? The contrast would have been unlivable. Simon Peter, faced with a notably lesser revelation, cried out: "'Depart from me,... O Lord!" For he was astonished' (Lk 5:8-9). God was leading her carefully and considerately, 'with cords of compassion, with the bands of love' (Hos 11:4).

The child who had brought her joy was gradually to become a source of anguish. Simeon foretold a sword which would pierce her soul (Lk 2:35). This piercing is not only that of the sorrow that ran her through on Calvary. The context, it would seem, speaks of a laceration of the spirit just as much as of the heart, where the sword does not strike only from outside. Mary does not doubt, indeed, she knows, but she does not understand and her spirit is torn apart. Jesus in the same way knows and says: 'Abba, Father!' And yet he does not comprehend, and cries out in anguish: 'Abba, Father, all things are possible to thee; remove this cup from me' (Mk 14:36); 'Why hast thou forsaken me?' (Mk 15:34). It is often said that Mary had to follow the path of the faith, as we have to; but more than we do she underwent the martyrdom of faith, when man dies to himself – until the Easter day when death was transformed into resurrection, when questions no longer needed to be asked (Jn 16:23), when the mother was able to believe in the luminous joy of the Spirit, in whom she is mother and who teaches all things (cf Jn 14:29).

Nevertheless her long meditation continued. Henceforth, it was not only 'all these things' that Mary kept in her heart (Lk 2:19, 51): it was Christ himself. Jesus ascended to the Father and came mysteriously alive among those who were his own: 'I go away and I will come to you' (Jn 14:28). His presence is different, something that is new both for him and for those who are his own: 'In that day you will know that I am in my Father, and you in me, and I in you' (Jn 14:20). Paul says of himself: 'It is no longer I who live, but Christ who lives in me' (Gal 2:20) and affirms this of all who believe (cf 1 Cor 1:30). Born of Mary by the power of the Spirit, Jesus is once again present in her in an ineffable manner through the same Spirit by whom the Father raises up the Son in the heart of those who believe. Like the Apostle and undoubtedly to a greater extent than he, she can say: 'Christ lives in me.' The risen Son is the source from which the Spirit springs up in the Church (Jn 7:39): it is he who henceforth gives his mother the Spirit by whom she became his mother.

The Acts of the Apostles shows the mother of Jesus among the disciples who 'devoted themselves to prayer' (Acts 1:14) and on whom the Spirit was to descend. It is the last picture scripture offers us of Mary in her earthly life. This presence in prayer at the heart of the infant Church opens up new vistas for our meditation before the Icon. Mary, icon of the Holy Spirit, is also the figure of the Church.

But before following this path would it not be a good idea to halt for a moment just to contemplate the holy image? Theologians seek to pin down the truth of a wonderful mystery; but they cannot succeed in expressing its beauty and thus betray even its truth. In their too heavy hands the crystal breaks into a splintering of ideas: withered by dry conceptualizations, the rose loses its petals. Who apart from poets and writers can evoke the girl whom God himself invited to joy, this mother of the Son of God whom no-one would have been able to invent if the Father had not created her? The Holy Spirit who overshadowed Mary has also descended on some Christians to inspire them. We do fortunately have poets and writers.

Here is Charles Péguy in his *Le Porche du mystère de la deuxième vertu*:

All creatures lack something, and not just the fact that they are not the Creator.

Those that are carnal lack, as we know,
the gift of purity.
But those that are pure, it should be
realized, lack carnality.
Only one being is pure while also being
carnal.
Only one being is carnal while also being
pure.
That is why the Blessed Virgin is not
merely the greatest blessing that lighted
on earth.
But the greatest blessing that ever
descended on the whole of creation.
She is not only the first among all women,
blessed among women.
She is not only the first among all creatures.
She is a creature who is unique and
infinitely, infinitely exceptional.

Here is Georges Bernanos in his *Diary of a
country priest*:[33]

The ancient world of sorrow, the world
before the access of grace, cradled her in
its heavy heart for many centuries, dimly
awaiting a *virgo genitrix*. For centuries and
centuries those ancient hands, so full of
sin, cherished the wondrous girl-child
whose name even was unknown. A little
girl, the queen of the Angels! And she's
still a little girl, remember!...
The Virgin was Innocence. Think what

we must seem to her, we humans. Of course she hates sin, but after all she has never known it, that experience which the holiest saints have never lacked, St Francis of Assisi included, seraphic though he was. The eyes of Our Lady are the only real child-eyes that have ever been raised to our shame and sorrow. Yes, lad, to pray to her as you should you must feel those eyes upon you: they are not indulgent – for there is no indulgence without something of bitter experience – they are eyes of gentle pity, wondering sadness, and with something more in them, never yet known or expressed, something which makes her younger than sin, younger than the race from which she sprang and though a mother, by grace, Mother of all grace, the youngest of the human family.

And here is Marie Noël in her *Notes intimes*:

Yesterday evening I treated myself to a little walk to the ante-room of Paradise... Yesterday evening, 8 September, I went to Benediction in that wonderful Lady chapel in the cathedral, the one that gives the impression of flying away...

There, in the drowsy blue of the stained-glass windows, I meditated without wanting to on the grace of the Blessed Virgin – oh, not her theological grace –

just her gentle grace of heart, of her smile, of surrender, of simplicity, of tenderness. What a delightful girl the Blessed Virgin must have been!

NOTES

1. Donatien Mollat, S.J., in *Dictionary of Biblical Theology*, ed. Xavier Léon-Dufour, London, 1967, p. 177.

2. With regard to the text of 1 Peter 4:14 established by textual criticism as 'the spirit of glory and of God', some good manuscripts have the reading 'the spirit of glory and of power, the spirit of God.'

3. St Augustine, *On the Trinity*, 8:14, CCL 50:290.

4. St Maximilian Kolbe, *L'Immaculée révèle l'Esprit Saint*, trans. J. F. Villepelée, Paris, 1974, p. 48.

5. That is to say in an action that is at once single and combined.

6. The Spirit is the heavenly reality: cf John 3:5, where Jesus glosses the phrase 'born from above' as 'born of water and the Spirit'.

7. In John 3:5, 6, 8 the same preposition is used to state that the children of God are born of the Spirit.

8. Out of respect for the name of God it was not used and the biblical writers evoked God's action by making use of what exegetes have called the 'divine passive'.

9. Everything that theologians say of the divine nature is to be found personalized in the Holy Spirit. That is why I allow myself to say that the Spirit is like the bosom where the Father feeds the eternal Son. Cf. my little work T*he Spirit of the Father and of the Son*, St Paul Publications, Slough, 1990.

10. It seems that a Jew never used in his prayers the invocation 'Abba' that belongs above all to the language of a child talking to its father. For Jesus, this mode of address was normal.

11. The bull *Ineffabilis* which defined Mary's Immaculate Conception calls Christ *'communis Dei Patris et Virginis Filius'* the Son jointly of God the Father and of the Virgin: DS2801.

12. Mary is described as being exempted from the stain of original sin by virtue of the foreseen merits of Christ. God could thus have exempted any man or woman of the Old Testament by virtue of this anticipation of the merits of Christ.

13. According to Romans 5:5-17 the grace the believer finds in Christ is much greater than the evil brought about by the sin of Adam. One can thus say that the grace of Christ in every believer is a greater good than being exempt from the stain of original sin.

14. To talk in this way is not to deny original sin, but merely to refrain from placing it at man's absolute origin.

15. Already we find this in St Justin, *Dialogue with Trypho* 78, and Origen, *Contra Celsum* 1:51.

16. The Semitic phrase 'blessed among women' corresponds to our superlative.

17. The Messianic interpretation of this passage is ancient, and is indeed suggested by the Septuagint translation which, like the RSV quoted here, uses 'he' rather than 'she' or 'it'.

18. I have substituted 'towards' for the RSV's 'for' to indicate the meaning of the Greek preposition *eis*.

19. I indicated this some time ago in my book *The Resurrection: A biblical study*, London and New York, 1960, pp. 98-103.

20. Jean Guitton, *Un siècle, une vie*, Paris, 1988, pp. 188-189, quotes this remark by Teilhard de Chardin which he regards as sibylline: 'Having set out from childhood to discover the heart of matter, it was inevitable that one day I should find myself face to face with the feminine.' The relationship between the two seems evident.

21. Cf. the Feast of the Presentation.

22. G. Bernanos, *Diary of a country priest*, London, 1937: Fount edition (Glasgow, 1977), p. 181.

23. The Greek term *kecharitomene* does not mean only 'she who is the object of grace', 'full of grace'. As Ignace

de la Potterie has shown in *Marie dans le mystère de l'Alliance*, Paris, 1988, pp. 52-53 and more fully in *Biblica* 69 (1987) pp. 357-382 and 480-508, the verb *charitoo* has a causative sense, just as similar verbs do: for example *eleutheroo* means to liberate, *leûkoo* means to whiten. 'They indicate an action that brings something about...' Mary is not only the object of divine favour, she is 'transformed by this grace'.

24. When it is said: 'You were bought with a price' (1 Cor 6:20, 7:23) God is the subject of the action expressed by the verb in the passive: it is he who pays the great price by begetting his Son for us in the world. 'God so loved the world that he gave his only Son' (Jn 3:16). He gave him by begetting him for us in the world.

25. John Paul II, *A l'image de Dieu, homme et femme*, Paris, 1980, pp. 32-33: '... the situation of original innocence and original sin. These two dimensions have their own dimension in man in his inmost core, in his knowledge, in his conscience, in his choices and in his decisions.'

26. Christ associates with men and women who are sinners not in their capacity as sinners, since he 'knew no sin' (2 Cor 5:21). The world in which the Son became incarnate is not radically sinful: it is even in harmony with him, having been created in him and towards him. It is however in their condition of weakness and death that he associates with them, where they 'fall short of the glory of God' (Rom 3:23) and are in need of salvation. He took 'the form of a servant' (Phil 2:7), that of a prodigal son far from his father's house. Out of the existential estrangement in which he finds himself, sinful man has made a state of having broken with God which is the sign of his condemnation. For Christ this estrangement is the place of his submission to the Father. He lives this to the extremity of estrangement and submission, in obedience unto death (Phil 2:8), where he finds himself in full communion with the Father. Glorified for ever at this extremity, in the very mystery of his death, he is for ever in solidarity with the world which he must lead to salvation.`

We see that Christ is at the heart of the sinful world thanks to his very holiness. This lets us say that it is through the holiness which nevertheless distinguishes her from it that Mary is in solidarity with the sinful world.

27. See my book *L'Esprit Saint de Dieu*, Paris, 1983, pp. 37, 59, 94, 121-122, 132, 146, 161: English translation, *Holy Spirit of God: an essay in biblical theology*, London, 1986.

28. Is this the reason why the child is carried to surround its mother with the nimbus of virginity?

29. The reader will have recognized here a tendency that belongs to Protestant thinking.

30. 'Ultimately the soul designates the person', Xavier Léon-Dufour in *Dictionary of Biblical Theology*, London, 1967, p. 496.

31. St Augustine, *Sermo 13 in Nativitate Domini*, PL 38:1019.

32. Cf. J. Pintard, *'Le principe "prius in mente quam corpore" dans la patristique et la théologie latine'*, in *Le Saint-Esprit et Marie*, III, Bulletin de la société française d'études mariales, 1970, pp. 25-28.

33. Fount edition, pp. 179-181.

Part 2

ICON OF THE CHURCH

9

Where things meet

In interpreting and applying to Mary the 'great portent' that 'appeared in heaven' (Rev 12:1) our procedure did not follow the logical order. We started with what, in interpreting this text, should have come at the end. But why not start at the end sometimes? In the history of salvation the end explains the beginnings: it is the fullness that gives sense and meaning to the whole.

The woman clothed with the sun is, on the first level of interpretation, the symbol of the Church. The number of the stars with which she is crowned is a convincing proof of this. The numbers used in such profusion in the Book of Revelation are cyphers which every informed reader would know how to decode (cf Rev 13:18): twelve, with its multiples, is the ecclesial number that indicates the Church (cf Rev 21:14).

But the Church is not a collectivity, a conglomeration of individuals: that which is the 'bride of the Lamb', beloved and loving, takes shape in a community of persons bound to Christ and to each other by the bond of the Holy Spirit. It is individualized and personalized in each believer and is to be found in each, in different degrees of perfection. It has been possible to say '*Ecclesia in singulis tota*', the whole Church is to be found in its individual parts.[34]

The woman crowned with the twelve stars, the mother of Christ, is the symbol of the Church of the first covenant,[35] which bore in its flesh the Messiah to come. She is also the symbol of the Church of the New Testament which, after the birth of Christ, gave birth to 'the rest of her offspring' (Rev 12:17). Now it is in the person of Mary that Israel gave birth to Christ. It is also to Mary that Jesus says, pointing to the beloved disciple: 'Behold, your son!' (Jn 19:26). The Church of the first covenant and that of the final covenant meet in Mary and find their expression in her. One could say '*Ecclesia tota in Maria*', the whole Church is in Mary.

The icon of the Spirit, Mary is thus also the icon of the Church. But it is in a different way. The Spirit is like the divine womb in which God begets his Son and those who are united with him: it takes Mary up into this role and enables her to play it in a human way. From the Spirit she receives her identity of *Theotokos*, God-bearer: it is the Spirit who makes her its icon. The Church does not confer on Mary her identity as mother and does not enable her to be the icon of the Church. On the contrary, it is in Mary that the Church's vocation of motherhood finds its fulfilment. The Church too is a mother in the fecundity of the Spirit; but it is first of all in Mary that this motherhood is realized. Mary is the icon of the Church because it is in her that we find, personalized, all the mystery of the Church as in no other member of the Church.

10
The Church of the first covenant

The writer of the Book of Revelation casts a prophet's glance over the history of the past and plumbs its invisible depths. He considers the Church of the first covenant in the image of a woman who has always borne Christ in her womb. Another prophet, the apostle Paul, in the same way found in the Bible, beyond the surface realities which he called 'the letter', the presence of Christ which is its 'spirit', the profound and consistent reality.

Christ's presence in mankind goes back to the dawn of time. The ancient serpent that stood before the pregnant woman waiting for the child that he might devour it is the serpent of the terrestrial paradise (Rev 12:4, 9). The Church of Christ existed since then, symbolized by the first woman in whom was deposited, like a seed, the promise of the Messiah (cf Gen 3:15). Through an advent that lasted for millennia, this distant ancestress bore Christ: it was already Christian but in the flesh, formed of those who in their flesh were bound to the body of the Christ who was to come. The definition of the Church as the body of Christ (cf Eph 1:22-23) already applied, but differently. Ever since it was crying out in the pains of childbirth, throughout its tormented history.

In the person of Eve the promise is intended for the whole of mankind. Gradually it focused on smaller and smaller ethnic groups. God's concern focused on a race, that of Shem (Gen 9:26); on a people, that of Abraham (Gen 15:4-6); on a tribe, that of Judah (Gen 49:10); on a clan, that of David (2 Sam 7:14). The promise is honed down and the group of people to whom it applies shrinks: a prophetic pyramid is built looking for its summit.

Israel is a maternal nation. Blessings are granted to the descendants of Abraham. God promises: 'I will raise up your offspring after you, who shall come forth from your body' (2 Sam 7:12); 'I will raise up for David a righteous Branch' (Jer 23:5). Already the sign of salvation is that 'a young woman shall conceive and bear a son' (Is 7:14), 'until the time when she who is in travail has brought forth' (Mic 5:3). The Messianic promises are given to the womb of 'the daughter of Zion'.

The nation thus bore hidden within it the Christ that was to be. God made his promises to Abraham and his descendants (Gen 15:15-16). St Paul is aware that this offspring will be as many as the dust of the earth; but, basing his argument on the fact that the word is used in the singular, he states that it is only Christ who is meant by the promise: 'It does not say, "And to offsprings," referring to many; but, referring to one, "And to your offspring," which is Christ' (Gal 3:16). The Apostle sees the offspring of Abraham contained and summed up in this single descendant.

According to Galatians 4:29 Isaac, the son of the promise, bears the mark of the Christ who is to come. Born according to the flesh, he is nevertheless proclaimed 'child of the spirit'. For St Paul that which is related to Christ is 'spiritual' (cf 1 Cor 10:3-4), since Christ 'is the Spirit' (2 Cor 3:17) of the first covenant, he is its deepest reality.

The laughter which, according to Genesis 17:17, greeted the birth of Isaac is interpreted in John 8:56 as the expression of joy which makes Abraham thrill at the sight of Christ: 'Your father Abraham rejoiced that he was to see my day; he saw it and was glad.' In the miraculous birth of Isaac the patriarch rejoiced at the birth of his most illustrious descendant.

God proclaimed himself the father of one of the sons of David: 'I will raise up your offspring after you, who shall come forth from your body... I will be his father and he shall be my son' (2 Sam 7:12-14). The promise concerns Solomon and following him the entire line of David. But Jewish tradition interpreted it as applying to the last and greatest of David's sons (cf Ps 89); the Letter to the Hebrews (1:5) understands this sonship in the divine fullness of its meaning, which applies to Christ Jesus alone. This variety of possible interpretations means that the filial glory of the last of the line goes back to his ancestors, as far as Solomon.

Such was the grace and gift of interpretation that Jesus conferred on his disciples when 'he opened their minds to understand the scriptures' (Lk 24:45): in their sight he came alive in the history of the times before he was born and appeared to them in the reading of the Bible.

Israel was thus a maternal nation, blessed among the nations, which bore Christ in its womb: a Christian Church in its flesh. According to the Letter to the Ephesians (2:12) the pagans had been 'separated from Christ, alienated from the commonwealth of Israel and strangers to the covenants of promise'; this means that the Jewish people, on the other hand, possessed this privilege. Jesus was 'the substance of this people'.[36]

11

Mary, image of the first Church

A fifth-century bishop of Carthage commented in this way on the passage from the Book of Revelation: 'No one among you is unaware that the dragon is the devil, nor that the woman meant that Virgin Mary who, undefiled, brought forth our undefiled head. She indeed manifested in herself the image of the holy Church.'[37] It was Mary whom he saw in the first place in this symbol and secondarily the Church which she represented. He had the right to indulge in this inversion, since it is in Mary that the Church of the Old Testament, mother of Christ, reached its fulfilment.

The Messianic pyramid which was built up step by step from its very broad base (Gen 3:15) went from the race of Shem, the people of Abraham, the tribe of Judah, the clan of David, before it reached its summit and culmination in Mary. The lines converge in a single point: the first Church, Christian through its motherhood, comes to identify itself with Mary. *Rejoice*, God's messenger says to her (Lk 1:28): God's favour that rests on Israel because of the Son who is to be born rests on you.

Gabriel takes up the exhortation to rejoice that has so often been addressed to the daughter of Zion. He echoes the prophets and brings the invitation to her for whom it was always meant:

Rejoice greatly, O daughter of Zion!
Shout aloud, O daughter of Jerusalem!
Lo, your king comes to you (Zech 9:9).

And the angel said unto Mary:
'Hail, O favoured one, the Lord is with
    you!' (Lk 1:28).

Sing aloud, O daughter of Zion;
shout, O Israel!
Rejoice and exult with all your heart,
O daughter of Jerusalem!
The Lord has taken away the
    judgements against you,
he has cast out your enemies.
The King of Israel, the Lord, is in your
    midst;
you shall fear evil no more.
On that day it shall be said to Jerusalem:
'Do not fear, O Zion' (Zeph 3:14-16).

And the angel said unto Mary:
'Hail, O favoured one, the Lord is with
    you…
Do not be afraid, Mary, for you have
    found favour with God' (Lk 1:28, 30).

Isaiah foretold that the cloud of the glory of the Lord would rest on Zion: 'Then the Lord will create over the whole site of Mount Zion and over her assemblies a cloud by day, and smoke and the shining of a flaming fire by night' (Is 4:5). On that day when the Messiah was conceived the cloud of glory rested on the girl Mary, taking her under its shadow. Invited to rejoice, she sang: 'My soul magnifies the Lord' (Lk 1:46).

Was she fully aware of the immense favour shown to her in her being chosen? Would she have been able to live her very simple life if she had seen herself raised up all of a sudden to the culmination of her people's sacred history? But if she had been aware of it, it was not something she would have been able to boast about. She represented a nation which God came to save, born in the wilderness, found by God at the side of the dusty path, whom he washed and fed, whom he loved mercifully and adorned like a bride (Ezek 16:1-14). The woman crowned with the twelve stars also represents Eve to whom God showed mercy when he proclaimed the enmity between her and the serpent. Although she is holy and immaculate, in the sight of God she is the creature who invokes God's pity and to whom God answers: 'You have found favour' (Lk 1:30). Mary is mother through mercy, created in the salvation that God brings about in Christ.

* * *

Israel is sown by the word of God and begets in faith by this word. Abraham believed and his son is proclaimed the 'child of the Spirit' (Gal 4:29). His descendants are the children of the promise. The daughter of Zion is consecrated to God: she is mother by flesh and by faith in God who espouses her, mother in virginity. This is how the birth is proclaimed when Mary gives birth in faith and in the flesh. She is pre-eminently the daughter of Abraham the believer. 'Blessed is she who believed' (Lk 1:45) is what Elizabeth says to her: her merit was to have believed. Her virginal motherhood does not set her apart from the Jewish nation but places her at the heart and the apex of her people. The word was at work in her more than in Sarah and all her ancestresses: the conception of the child was more miraculous, and the need for faith in the God of the impossible was greater (cf Lk 1:37).

From its beginnings Christian faith per-ceived the presence of Christ in the Old

Testament. Later the Christian heart, loving and praying, came to understand that the praise accorded by the Bible to the daughter of Zion was intended above all for the mother of Jesus, in whom it found its supreme justification. If God established enmity between the serpent and Eve, her distant ancestress, did not this saying of Genesis apply to Mary, proclaiming enmity all the sharper in that Mary more than Eve is the mother of the Messiah? At the feast of the Immaculate Conception the Church says of her: 'He has clothed me with the garments of salvation, he has covered me with the robe of righteousness' (Is 61:10). It addresses to her the praise bestowed on Judith, the national heroine who by her very name of 'the Jewess' evokes the entire nation: 'You are the exaltation of Jerusalem, you are the great glory of Israel, you are the great pride of our nation!' (Jud 15:19). In proclaiming: 'Blessed are you among women, and blessed is the fruit of your womb!' (Lk 1:42) Elizabeth was applying to Mary the praise bestowed on Judith: 'You are blessed by the Most High God above all women on earth; and blessed be the Lord God' (Jud 13:18). Mary is the city of God of which 'glorious things are spoken' (Ps 87:3). The faithful proclaim her 'queen of patriarchs' because it is through this girl that they became ancestors worthy of veneration; 'queen of prophets' because it was of her womb that they foretold the blessed fruit. She was indeed herself a prophet and more so than the rest of them. Formerly the 'men of the spirit' (Hos 9:7) proclaimed a multitude of sayings (cf Heb 1:1), but it was Mary who brought the unique Word forth into the world, by the power of the Spirit. Mary was a prophet through her entire being as a mother, just as the entire Church of the first covenant is the proclamation of final salvation.

This young Jewess will always remain the glory of Israel. In her the Church of today honours the people of the first covenant: God, looking on her, has remembered 'Abraham and his posterity for ever' (Lk 1:55). The cloud of light and glory rests eternally on the daughter of Zion.

12

The Church in Jesus' passover

The day came when the child was to be born, to be carried away to be with God: 'She was with child and she cried out in her pangs of birth… She brought forth a male child,… but her child was caught up to God and to his throne' (Rev 12:2,5).

It was known that the Messianic age would be born in the pangs of childbirth. These tribulations have traversed the centuries: from the beginning, the woman who was with child has been crying out in her labour pains (Rev 12:1-4). The writer of the Book of Revelation compresses the entire trajectory of Christ's coming and what he achieved into the miraculous conjunction of a painful birth and glorification with God.

It is the child on whom have descended the pangs of childbirth of the last age: 'Was it not necessary that the Christ should suffer these things and enter into his glory?' (Lk 24:26). But in the Book of Revelation it is the sufferings of the mother that symbolize the Messianic trials, since the community is inseparable from the child she is bearing in her flesh. She shares the sufferings through which the child is born to be with God (cf Jn 16:21).

Jesus is the point where the Old and New Testaments meet: the end of the one, the beginning of the other, and the transition from the one to the other. His 'flesh is the hinge of salvation.'[38] He passes from the flesh to the Spirit and carries the Church with him in this passover. In him the Church of the first covenant finds its conclusion: it dies in him, with a death that does not do away with it but leads it to its ultimate truth.

It dies. Formed of those who, in the flesh, are united to Christ in his flesh, it breathes its last on the cross with Christ, who from the flesh passes into the realms of the Spirit. During his life on earth, Jesus, 'born of woman, born under the law' (Gal 4:4), belonged to a considerable extent to the first covenant. He was reduced to 'the form of a servant' (Phil 2:7) where the mystery of his Sonship was hidden: externally he seemed no more than a man (cf Phil 2:7). Yet he had to 'depart... to the Father' (Jn 13:1), to whom he was all the same united in the depths of his being (Jn 10:30). It was thus that he appeared in the flesh to a people who were living 'according to the flesh' while being energized by the Spirit: in the form of a slave while being destined for Sonship (Gal 4:1-3). But on the cross Jesus died to the flesh, to the law (cf Gal 2:19), to his being enclosed within this earthly people: from now on he lives in his Father (Rom 6:10), in the Holy Spirit: 'Descended from David according to the flesh and designated Son of God in power according to the Spirit of holiness by his resurrection from the dead' (Rom 1:3-4). 'Her child was caught up to God and to his throne' (Rev 12:5).

That is the work of salvation: 'Through the curtain, that is, through his flesh' (Heb 10:20) 'he entered once for all into the Holy Place,... thus securing an eternal redemption' (Heb 9:12).

During the first covenant 'the woman' had been the mother of Christ according to the flesh: within herself she bore him who was 'the substance of this people'. But by the cross Christ left the flesh for the spirit. From now on his life is different. He said: 'Destroy this temple' (Jn 2:19), 'this temple that is made with hands' (Mk 14:58). At Jesus' death the veil of the Temple was torn, 'your house is forsaken and desolate' (Mt 23:38). The first covenant dies with him.

But this temple Jesus raises up again in a new form: 'But he spoke of the temple of his body' (Jn 2:21). Between one temple and the other, between one covenant and the other, there is a breach ('Destroy this temple'), while at the same time a continuity prevails ('and in three days I will raise it up') in something that is completely new. This pattern of breach and continuity is first of all proper to Christ in his earthly existence and his transformed life of glory. The Church of God gathers in the rebuilt temple, in communion with Christ dead to the flesh and raised up in the Spirit.

It thus finds itself formed once again of a gathering of men and women united to the body of Christ, but the bond is no longer in the flesh. In his death to the flesh Jesus carries with him the nation that was his mother and the whole of mankind. Formerly mother according to the flesh, the Church becomes the companion of Jesus' passover: like a wife who forms one body with him, she falls asleep with him in his death and awakens with him in his resurrection.[39]

13
Mary in Jesus' passover

'Standing by the cross of Jesus was his mother' (Jn 19:25). Whether she was aware of it or not, she represents the Church of the first covenant. Thus gathered around the cross were the patriarchs, the prophets and all the just men and women of old. Despite its present leaders Israel is faithful, in the person of Mary: with her Israel enters into the new covenant.

Right from the start Mary's motherhood was marked with the sign of Easter. God gave her her Son and at the same time took him away. Every mother has to part with her child to bring him or her into the world: this maternal duty weighed more than on any other on the mother who was 'blessed among all women'. This was because it was only through death that her son was to come to his full birth as Son.

Luke's gospel does not talk of Mary's presence by the cross. But in his gospel Calvary was outlined on the horizon of Jesus' childhood. In Israel every first-born belongs to Yahweh: his parents have to redeem him for him to be their child (Ex 13:2,11-13). Now Jesus is taken to the temple not to be redeemed but 'to present him to the Lord' (Lk 2:22). This is because 'the child to be born of you will be called holy' (Lk 1:35), consecrated for ever. The carrying away of the child to be with God (Rev 12:5) begins right from his earthly birth, to be fulfilled one day in a total separation. Such is the entire birth of Jesus, and thus far does Mary's relationship of motherhood with him extend.

That is why the human bonds between the Son and his mother are not slow to be loosened: 'Did you not know that I must be in my Father's house?' (Lk 2:49). A family takes shape around Jesus united to him by the bond of faith alone: 'My mother and my brothers are those who hear the word of God and do it' (Lk 8:21). A woman cries out: 'Blessed is the womb that bore you, and the breasts that you sucked!' But for his part he says: 'Blessed rather are those who hear the word of God and keep it!' (Lk 11:27-28). From now on faith must take precedence over the flesh. In Mary's eyes the features of her Jesus disappear and all that can now be seen is the countenance of the anointed one of God, the Christ.

It is the Father who draws his Son to him and thus removes him from his mother and from Israel. But he is always faithful to Israel and to the gift given to Mary, and associates them with his Son whom by death he raises up to be with him.

Using a characteristic technique,[40] John announces the final hour at the start of his gospel: 'O woman, what have you to do with me? My hour has not yet come' (Jn 2:4).[41] The hour of Jesus, that of his passover, is also that of the Church in its transition from the old to the new covenant. At Cana Jesus did the first of his signs, which were all proclamations of this hour. The evangelist notes as an important circumstance: 'The mother of Jesus was there' (Jn 2:1). She is not given her name of Mary: she is 'the mother of Jesus' whom Jesus addresses by the unusual term: 'woman!' The two terms suit Mary: she is the woman, the mother, the symbol of the nation of the covenant. The young couple at Cana are only there as the setting: the action takes place between Jesus and his mother against the background of a wedding feast. The mother notices the lack of wine: 'They have no wine' (Jn 2:3). A superabundance of wine characterizes the Messianic age (Is 25:6; Joel 2:24, 3:18; Amos 9:13-14), and they have none. Faithful and obedient, she tells the servants: 'Do whatever he tells you' (Jn 2:5).

The six jars contained water meant for the purification rites of the old covenant (Jn 2:6); John the Baptist baptized in water and was not capable of baptizing in the Spirit (Jn

1:33). And here we have Jesus announcing the time of the Holy Spirit when wine abounds in plenty and more than plenty: he proclaims the transition from the law that came from Moses to the rule of grace and truth (Jn 1:17).[42] The glory of Easter begins to dawn, the faith of Easter begins to be born: 'This, the first of his signs, Jesus did at Cana in Galilee and manifested his glory; and his disciples believed in him' (Jn 2:11). Cana is the first stage towards the hour when the first Church passes over into that of the covenant in the Holy Spirit. 'The mother of Jesus was there', the woman who gave birth to Jesus and who is the symbol of Israel.

This woman who was present when everything began is found again by the evangelist at the cross: 'Standing by the cross of Jesus was his mother' (Jn 19:25).

> Completely wounded,
> profoundly fulfilled,
> at the foot of the triumphal tree
> here is the Church upright
> looking on her first-born.[43]

Such is Jesus' mother at Calvary: 'the Church upright', parallel to the cross of the Son, united to him in rising up to the Father through death. In the person of Mary the Church passes from the first to the new covenant, together with Christ.

The evangelist emphasized Mary's docility at Cana: 'Do whatever he tells you.' It is futile to mention it again now: she is there, in obedient and painful communion with the Son in his death. Jesus left her long ago to find her again when his hour came.

The only Son dies, the earthly link with his mother is broken: the first covenant, based on Christ in his flesh, dies at this moment. In the person of Mary Israel according to the flesh and to faith is obedient to God until death. Thus is inaugurated the new Church of which it is said: 'Do you not know that all of us who have been baptized into Christ Jesus were baptized into his death?' (Rom 6:3). In Mary standing by the cross of Jesus the Church of the first covenant is transformed into the new Church.

The Church of the past is not destroyed but fulfilled: 'I have come not to abolish but to fulfil' (Mt 5:17). At Cana the jars of water were not emptied to make way for wine: the water itself was transformed, ennobled. In the same way Jesus' earthly life is not denied in the resurrection but reaches its culmination in eternity, in the death in which Christ is glorified.[44] And Mary does not stop being the mother of Jesus: after the resurrection of the Son, 'the mother of Jesus' was there among the disciples. Her motherhood is exercised in new dimensions.

14
Associated with the Saviour

In the order of earthly things Mary and the Church preceded Christ: they bore him in their flesh and brought him forth. In his passover of death and resurrection Jesus assumes the headship of mankind, whose future he is: Mary and the Church follow him, associated with his passover.

Jesus is the mystery of salvation in person: 'Christ Jesus, whom God made our ... redemption' (1 Cor 1:30), 'he became the source of eternal salvation to all who obey him' (Heb 5:9), at one and the same time the saviour and the event of salvation. In his passover he is our passover. This is something he owes neither to his mother nor to the Church: it is according to his Father's will that he dies for our redemption and rises again in the Spirit, so that we may come to fullness of life in him (Col 2:9-10).

But if it is true that he is the one and only saviour, it is by associating men and women with himself that he leads them to the salvation that has been realized in his person. Jesus has become 'a life-giving Spirit' (1 Cor 15:45), he has been transformed into the mode of existence of the Holy Spirit, he has become an infinitely open being capable of taking the multitude up into what is personal to him, his death and resurrection. It is in this way that he really 'died and was raised' for us (2 Cor 5:15), his death and resurrection becoming ours in our communion with him. St Paul states firmly that the Christian puts on Christ (Gal 3:27), becomes a single body with him, in the same death and the same resurrection (Rom 6:3-6, Col. 2:12). The Christian is saved by communion in the mystery of salvation, saved therefore in sharing in the salvation of the world. The Apostle knows that his communities benefit from his own participation in Christ's death and resurrection (2 Cor 4:10-12).

The Church has the grace of being at one and the same time saved and saving, sanctified and sanctifying, together with Christ, the unique saviour. It does not add anything but receives everything: it does not provide any addition but shares in everything. It is like the vine of which Christ is the root.

Mary, the companion of Christ at Calvary, is the image of the Church associated with the Saviour and which, in communion with him, is the mother of those who believe.[45]

15
The mother of believers

Having given birth to the only Son, the
woman clothed with the sun experienced an
extraordinary fertility (cf Rev 12:17).

The psalmist had already contemplated in
the Zion of the Messiah the city of all the
peoples (Ps 87:5-7):

> And of Zion it shall be said,
> 'This one and that one were born in
>   her';
> for the Most High himself will establish
>   her.
> The Lord records as he registers the
>   peoples,
> 'This one was born there.'
> Singers and dancers alike say,
> 'All my springs are in you.'

Taken up into heaven in Jesus' passover,
the Messianic Jerusalem becomes 'the Jerusalem above,... our mother' (Gal 4:26). The
first Christians called this heavenly Jerusalem
'the virgin mother'.[46] It is truly a mother: not

only does it teach, guide and feed, but it gives birth. It gives birth as a spouse, in union with its Lord: 'He who abides in me and I in him, he it is that bears much fruit' (Jn 15:5). It is like the vine of which Christ is the rootstock. It is united to him by communion of death and resurrection and shares in the fecundity of the Spirit which makes of Christ 'a life-giving spirit' (1 Cor 15:45), a being that is the source of being.

Because Mary is the symbol and summary of the Church, the grace of universal motherhood is given to her first of all.

'As Father of the world to come, [Christ] by preference links himself to her and becomes with her, for the whole body of the Church, a principle of divine generation. In this way, having received from God in his resurrection the gift of having life in himself in order to bestow it on all men and women and to justify them by the substance of divine justice which is in him, he takes for his helper the most blessed virgin as a new Eve; and at the same time he puts her in communion with all that he has received from his Father, to make her mother of the living.

'Wonder of wonders: everything that Jesus Christ will achieve, from the moment of the formation of the Church to the last judgement, he has formed in his mother... I am not surprised that St John has understood better than anyone else the holy and glorious mystery of the Church of God, because he had always before him the most blessed virgin, in which he saw the entire Church enclosed and epitomized.'[47]

Jesus is the only Son. But God begets him in the world so as to include all men and women in this unique begetting. Jesus is the Son-of-God-for-us; God for us is Father of the Only-begotten; the Spirit for us is the power of divine conception in Mary. She for us is the mother of this Son. The words addressed to her on Calvary are a seal of authenticity: they certify that Mary is in all truth the mother of Jesus, who is Son-of-God-for-us.

Mary has been called mediatrix of graces. This title could be deceptive, making people think that God hands grace over to Christ the mediator who hands it on to Mary who for her part hands it out. Mary is mother: mediatrix is another and more abstract name for her spiritual motherhood. A mother does not bestow life by handing it out. She is in a communion of life with the child conceived within her and feeds the child from her own being.

More than something that one possesses and that can be handed out, grace is communion. It ennobles man by raising him up to the mode of being of the triune God, where everything is relationship and mutual self-giving. It makes of everyone a being who is open, showing solidarity and at the same time giving oneself, binding people to each other and mutually enriching them. It is in this way that Jesus, the first, 'became a life-giving spirit' (1 Cor 15:45), given in his whole being and source of life to the extent that he is alive, a single body with the Church which he consecrates to God in his own paschal consecration (Jn 17:19). Whoever lives 'in Christ' shares his mode of being-with-people and being-for-people: such people also become themselves 'life-giving spirits' who sanctify those to whom they are united, to the extent of their own sanctification. Grace creates the communion of saints.

Mary's place is at the heart of this communion, through the fullness of holiness that has been granted to her. That is the meaning of her title of mediatrix.

Grace is thus fraternal, because it puts people in communion with each other, and also maternal, because it makes each person a source of life. Mary is our universal sister through the grace of fullness that unites her with everyone: she is also the mother of everyone through this fullness with which she is filled. Grace is this, fraternal and maternal, because it is sharing in the mode of being of the Holy Spirit who is at one and the same time the bond of love and the divine fecundity.[49]

The communion of saints, like everything

that concerns the Holy Spirit and love, is a mystery: it baffles rational analysis. However, because they have some experience of love, people know that love binds one person to another, enabling them to share and draw on the other's riches. It is in this way that a prince who marries a girl from a humble background turns her into a princess by the fact of marrying her. But to a greater extent than human love the Spirit, who is a creative love, creates a community where everyone is rich from the person of the other. Christ raises to his level the Church to which he gives himself: he makes of it his own body by loving it, sanctifying it in his own holiness. Someone who is loved by a saint is linked to heaven by the love with which he or she is loved. Through the saint bound to him or her in love he or she forms part of the kingdom of God, he or she is the object of God's grace. It is in this way that St Paul can affirm that the spouse who remains an unbeliever is sanctified by his or her spouse who has become a Christian, by virtue of the conjugal love that binds them together (1 Cor 7:12-14). For his part St Thomas Aquinas writes: 'If we presuppose a relationship of love with someone else, then one can desire and hope for something for this other person, as for oneself. And in keeping with this someone can hope for eternal life for another, to the extent that the one is united to the other by love.'[49]

Mary is the icon of the maternal Church because she is the icon of the Spirit of love: she is mediatrix by the holiness of love which binds her to all who believe. Thanks to this bond of love, they are loved by God, they form part of the community of saints where the grace of the Holy Spirit reigns. Mary is mediatrix through the universal love which the Spirit places in her heart.

All true Christians are mediators of graces: they sanctify others in the power of the charity that sanctifies themselves. The privilege of mediation thus does not separate Mary from the community and raise her up above it: her privilege is that of an incomparable charity which distinguishes her by placing her at the heart of the maternal Church. In her the communion of saints is brought to its highest degree of intensity.

No-one else can ever exceed or even reach this height, since in Mary the motherhood of souls is based on the unshareable grace of being the mother of him who is Son-of-God-for-all. Mary thus does not derive her privilege from belonging to the Church that mediates graces. Of course, she is not above the Church, she forms part of the family, but she is not just an ordinary member: in the family of the Church she is the mother of all.

Note that the mystery of the beginning when the Spirit overshadows Mary re-appears at the end, confirmed by Jesus' saying:

'Behold, your son!' (Jn 19:26). Mary is the mother of those who believe, mediatrix of graces, because she is the icon of the Spirit, through whom she became the mother of Jesus.

The Spirit is the fecundity of God, the womb in which God begets, in as much as it is the power of an infinite love: it is in loving without limit that God goes out of himself into his infinite Son; it is in his overflowing love that he begets in the world, in order to include the mass of humanity in the unique begetting of the Son. It is thus as the power of love that the Spirit overshadowed Mary. We must think that it began then to make her capable of loving such a Son, one who is Son of God for the mass of humanity. The trial of Calvary would have cloven the heart of the mother to an unfathomable depth, making of it a heart of infinite capacity, like the Messianic city of which the psalm sings, the city that is open to all the nations.

'When Christ who is our life appears' (Col 3:4), when the world experiences 'the power of his resurrection' (Phil 3:10) 'which enables him even to subject all things to himself' (Phil 3:21), then the mystery of the communion of saints will attain its supreme beatifying truth, Mary's maternal mediation will reach its fulfilment. This is because 'the power of his resurrection' is none other than the Holy Spirit, the power at one and the same time of infinite communion and of divine begetting.

'It is raised a spiritual body,' states the Apostle (1 Cor 15:44). Man will be transformed according to the mode of the Spirit, which is infinite communion and fecundity. In his passover Jesus 'became a life-giving spirit' (1 Cor 15:45), a being totally made up of self-giving and relationship. Now, 'when he appears we shall be like him' (1 Jn 3:2). Then the saying will be fully verified: 'As he is so are we' (1 Jn 4:17). Already on earth those who believe exist for each other: 'None of us lives to himself, and none of us dies to himself' (Rom 14:7). They live in holiness for each other and through each other. But how much more personal, how much more of a relationship will the existence of heaven be, lived in an intimate self-giving in a mutual giving of life.[50]

The resurrection of the dead is of course the work of the Father, in the begetting of the Only-begotten whom he raises up (cf Acts 13:33) and in whom he includes the mass of humanity: the Spirit is the vigour of this divine begetting, the womb in which the Father begets, the power of the resurrection. But the womb in which the mass of humanity is born is also the community which the Spirit fills with its presence: it is also Mary, icon of the Spirit, in whom the community finds itself 'enclosed and epitomized'.

Even in their glorified body the saints will

be children of 'the Jerusalem above,… our
mother' (Gal 4:26) and of Mary. Everything
comes from the Father through the Son in the
Holy Spirit and nevertheless everyone will be
able to say to the Church and to Mary: 'All my
springs are in you' (Ps 87:7).

16
Mary, the epitome of sacred history

Mary, in whom the mystery of the Church is summed up, is also the epitome of its long history. The trajectory that is spread over thousands of years is as it were contracted within the space of a single life. Mary's origins go back to the dawn of creation, when the Father ordains all things towards Christ: the conclusion of her life coincides with the end of the history of salvation. She is 'the creature in its initial honour and in its final flourishing.'[51] Between these two poles, these two extremes, she has traversed all the stages. God created her according to the model and the rhythm of the Spirit which is also itself at the beginning and at the end, since it is in it that the Father begets and that the Son is begotten, and it goes from one to the other. Again it is the Spirit who is the agent of the history of salvation.

Sacred history does not find its starting-point in the sin of Adam but in the moment when the Father creates all things towards his Son and in the mercy he showed to our first parents. It is also by this door that Mary enters into existence: in the moment when God creates with a view to the Christ who is to be born, when he puts enmity between the woman and the serpent (cf Gen 3:15). That is why the Catholic faith professes that Mary's conception was holy, immaculate, because of the Son who was to be born of her. The Church will reach its full stature on the day of the final resurrection: it is also in this ultimate grace that Mary's life finds its culmination. That is why the Catholic Church proclaims Mary's assumption into heaven. All the missions entrusted to the Church, from the beginning to the end, have been fulfilled by Mary. She bore within herself the Messianic seed planted in Israel, and it is through her that the Messiah was born. Like the new Church, she was associated with Jesus' passover, was made holy in this passover, and she is thus the mother of those who believe.

Mary is not only the figure of the Church, the exemplary daughter of Abraham and the model of Christianity: the Church which is individualized in varying degrees in each believer, depending on each one's fidelity, finds itself personalized, 'enclosed and epitomized' in Mary. This is because it is in her that the Church of the first covenant really bore Christ and gave birth to him; in her this Church died with Christ on the cross and passed into the new covenant; in her all the motherhood of the Church is summed up. The saying 'The whole Church is to be found in its individual parts' is only fully verified in Mary.

Nevertheless there is one aspect in which the Church does not see itself represented in Mary. The history of the Church tells of God's grace in the world, but also speaks of sins, of numerous sins. Mary, who lived in immediate communion with 'the Holy One of God (Jn 6:69) by whom the sin of the world has been taken away, is the image of the Church whose mystery is not being a sinner but being saved from sin. Mary is the image of the Church in the purity of its mystery.

That is why Mary does not cease to sing: 'My soul magnifies the Lord and my spirit rejoices in God my saviour' (Lk 1:46-47). The Church in its turn is full of gratitude, since in Mary it is completely faithful to its grace, 'without spot or wrinkle' (cf Eph 5:27), to the glory of God the Father (cf Eph 3:21).

However, her exceptional grace does not separate Mary either from the whole of creation or from the Jewish nation or from the new Church: her unique grace is universally shared; her privilege is that of the fullness which does not separate but which places Mary at the heart of the Church. She is holy in her origin, with all men and women who, before being born of the sinner Adam, are born of the Father, created in the Son and towards him. She is virgin and mother, like the primordial creation over which the Spirit broods, so that from the womb of the earth may be born Christ and the mass of humanity. She is virgin and mother with the Jewish nation which, by faith in the Word, bore within itself the Messianic seed; virgin and mother with every mother whose love, which brings about life, is a reflection of the virginal fertility of the Spirit. With the Church of the new covenant, Mary is mother of all who believe, in her communion of death and glory with Christ. Mary is among us, by all the grace which dwells in her.

This is why the Holy Spirit which inclines believers to love the Church also turns their hearts towards her in whom the Church finds itself completely. Anyone who judges excessive the loving veneration with which Mary is surrounded is unaware of the glory of God which burns at the heart of creation and which shines forth in the mystery of the Church. May God remove the blindfold from the eyes that do not see!

17
Living with Mary in the Church

'And from that hour the disciple took her to his own home' (Jn 19:27). In fact the text is saying more than that he merely lodged her in his own home, though that would have given him pleasure enough. He welcomed her into his own home as if she were his own mother.[52] Jesus did not ask him to put her up in his house but to welcome her in the relationship of mother and son: 'Behold, your mother!' The disciple regarded her as his mother; Mary regarded him as her son. For the second time this mother is aware of areas of love that are quite new opening up within her: as for the disciple, he learns how great the love is of his master, who allows him to be the son of his mother.

'And from that hour the disciple took her to his own home.' The hour involved is without a doubt that which John mentions frequently: the solemn hour when 'it is finished' (Jn 19:30).[53]

Jesus completes his work by founding the new Church, of which his mother is the symbol. The bond of motherhood and sonship which unites Mary and the disciple, the Church and those who believe, forms part of the hour, that is to say the work of salvation.

That is why one can imagine that filial love for Mary, like belonging to the Church, is for human beings a pledge or token of salvation. Those who effectively belong to the Church have their roots in the kingdom of heaven of which the Church, on earth, is the sacrament; those who love Mary are bound to the Church of which she is the symbol. The disciple's prayer and filial love for Mary, thus carry with them real promises of salvation. The Christian people, guided by a sure instinct, worked out a formerly well-known axiom. Its language may seem outdated today, but its truth is lasting: 'A servant of Mary cannot fail to obtain salvation.'[54] That is because the Marian devotee is united by means of prayer and love to her in whom God realizes a fullness of salvation.

It is true that one is saved by God's grace and in the welcome given to that grace: all the same, we receive grace within the Christian community which believes, loves, suffers and prays. What would have become of that brilliant young academic Aurelius Augustinus if his mother Monica had refused to pray for him at such length? Happy is every Christian who is surrounded by the prayer of another! If he or she is a sinner, even a great sinner, the loving prayer of his or her brother or sister will give him or her life: 'If any one sees his brother committing what is not a mortal sin, he will ask, and God will give him life' (1 Jn 5:16).

The sin this passage talks about may be very serious, but the brother who is a sinner will be restored to life, thanks to the prayer of the Church, provided that this sin 'is not mortal'. What is this saying? According to Johannine thinking mortal sin is that of unbelief or apostasy, heresy or voluntary schism or detestation of a brother, in other words a sin that creates a complete breach with God and the community.[55] But if the breach is not radical, fraternal prayer is capable of restoring life to the person concerned.[56]

For those who pray to Mary there is a Christian, a saint, the most holy of all and the most listened to by God, who as a true mother concerns herself with their salvation. Whether they are sinners and great sinners, as their sin is not mortal (since they pray, they maintain the bond of communion) they can be assured of salvation: on account of her who, for her part, prays for these people, with devotion and with an infallible power of intercession.

At the same time that grace is bestowed on such people, the welcome they should give grace is made easier. Grace is a seed and Marian prayer is the climate which allows it to germinate and grow.

This is because prayer to Mary is humble, like Mary herself. We are honouring a simple creature, for the glory of Christ, a woman whose life on earth did not create any stir.

> A woman about whom no-one said
>   anything,
> except that she had become engaged...
> A woman about whom no-one said
>   anything,
> except that she had given birth...
> A woman about whom no-one said
>   anything,
> except that she spent three days
>   searching...
> A woman about whom no-one said
>   anything,
> except that she was at Cana...
> A woman about whom no-one said
>   anything,
> except for her presence at the cross...
> A woman about whom no-one said
>   anything,
> except for her prayer with them.[57]

We are thus at the level of simple things, where God is close to man: 'Thou hast... revealed [these things] to babes' (Mt 11:25). God leans towards the side where his Holy

Spirit blows, and we know that the Spirit is 'the humility of God'.[58]

And the Spirit is love. All true love is humble with regard to the beloved. To pray to Mary is to love, at least with an initial love that will grow, it is to love with the love of a child with regard to its mother. Now the humility of a child possesses firm promises of salvation: 'He who humbles himself will be exalted' (Lk 14:11, 18:14). 'Little children do not damn themselves,' Teresa of Lisieux said gracefully and accurately.

Here as always Mary plays a role like that of the Church, of which she is the icon. Loving adherence to the community of the Church makes people humble and believing, welcoming and docile to grace. Those who reject the Church, who despise it, become hardened in pride: they are not the children of a mother.

There is more. When people pray to Mary, they open themselves to the longing for higher things, they put themselves in the disposition of those whom God wishes to save. This is because to long for higher things is already to possess them, to the extent that the longing is sincere. In fact, the Spirit is holy longing just as it is charity: the longing for heavenly things is the manifestation of its action in the human heart.

Icon of the Holy Spirit, creature of innocence and goodness, Mary attracts the human heart and draws it towards the heights. Among sinful humanity she is the younger sister who has never reached the age of sin, the primaeval paradise of honesty and gentleness found at last, the soft and guileless voice of childhood which is irresistible. This made Paul Verlaine say in his nostalgia for innocence: 'From now on I wish to love only my mother Mary.'[59] It has always been thought that prayer to Mary purifies a person's desires and longings.

At the same time there is lit the flame of hope, which is an initial glimmer of eternal life, a promise of the kingdom for whoever tends this flame. St Paul knows that hope will not be confounded, the sign of the Spirit poured into our hearts (cf Rom 5:5).

One thing was established in the past, in an age when people lived 'in Christendom': the sinner who was afraid of God, who fled from his countenance, could find hope through Mary. Charles Péguy did not dare say the Our Father because in it one says: 'Thy will be done.' He said the Hail Mary, because in that one asks: 'Pray for us sinners…'

Why sometimes does the mother of Jesus win somebody's confidence more easily than Christ? In the past people had a rather simplistic explanation: God had divided the kingdom into two parts, that of justice and that of mercy. Justice he had entrusted to the Son and mercy to his mother. Péguy once again echoes this view:

Because she is for mercy
and me – I really have to be for justice.[60]

That of course is not so. Mary does not possess any virtue which Christ does not have to perfection. But she is a simple creature and is not haloed with God's infinite majesty. That is why God is able to isolate in her certain aspects of his holiness and bring them into special relief. In Mary the charity of the Spirit is isolated from those aspects of supremacy it has in God.

Deprived of the connection with omnipotence and with God's justice – which the sinner wrongly regards as a kind of punitive and vindictive justice – the charity of the Spirit only manifests in her those traits of which every pure young girl and every true mother has a reflection: kindness and gentleness, a loving honesty that inclines them towards the child, the desire to love and to be loved, humble devotion and a readiness to forgive.

This same smile of God shines on the face of Christ: it is his mercy that makes Mary so sweet and kind. But it happens that men and women perceive it more easily on Mary's face, because this image of God expresses more naturally certain supreme refinements, certain subtleties of love that people only discover in God after a long life of intimacy with him but which they discover without trouble in her who is a woman so pure and who they know is their mother:

Because you are woman, the Eden of
    the old forgotten gentleness,
Whose look goes straight to the heart
    and makes the pent-up tears burst
    forth.[61]

This is why prayer to Mary is a prayer of last resort which people use or have recourse to when every other possibility of prayer seems to have disappeared.[62] Now those who pray are saved just as those who believe (Mk 16:16), since prayer – like faith, of which it is an expression – opens the heart to grace.

Mary has her dwelling among the lofty domains of the Spirit, where shines the sun of God in his love. Everyone is drawn towards these heights: created in the power of the Spirit who is love, they are made to love and to be loved. Mary and human beings, even great sinners, thus recognize that they are related: they are subject to the law of love. Now hope always brings rebirth, there where love exists. It will not be confounded or disappointed (Rom 5:5).

* * *

Those who believe contemplate the icon. But their look does not stop there however long they contemplate: the image does not make a screen, the mother leads to the Son. Otherwise would Mary be the icon of the Spirit and the icon of the Church?

The Spirit is pure relationship. It is the infinite power of loving which the Father issues from himself into his Son; his whole being is involved in the begetting of the Son. That is also the action of the Spirit in the world: by the power of the Spirit the Father begets the Son in the world and creates all things towards him. As for the Church which the Spirit impregnates with its presence, it is the sacrament of Christ, it is entrusted with taking men and women by the hand and leading them to the Saviour. Icon of the Spirit and of the Church, Mary is pure relationship to Christ: her identity is in motherhood with regard to Jesus. She only becomes someone's mother by the grace that makes of him or her a brother or sister of Christ.

That is why the Church calls Mary 'the gate of heaven that remains always open'.[63]

This heaven of which Mary is the gate is not some place that one might inhabit in the inter-stellar spaces. On earth, human happiness is to be found in relationships. This is also the happiness of God and of the saints. The Father builds his heaven for himself by begetting his Son in the power of love of the Spirit, this Son in whom he rests and is well-pleased. Of the Son he makes also heaven for human beings: he begets him for them in the world and encloses them in this unique begetting. Christ is heaven in person, built at the heart and at the apex of creation: heaven is our state of union with him. Did not Jesus state that with him the kingdom of heaven had come into the world? 'But if it is by the finger of God that I cast out demons, then the kingdom of God has come upon you' (Lk 11:20. 'Behold, the kingdom of God is in the midst of you' (Lk 17:21). Did he not promise the thief: 'Today you will be with me in paradise' (Lk 23:43)? And it is written in the Letter to the Ephesians: 'Blessed be the God and Father of our Lord Jesus Christ, who has blessed us in Christ with every spiritual blessing in the heavenly places... and made us sit with him in the heavenly places in Christ Jesus' (Eph 1:3, 2:6). To be in Christ is to dwell in heaven.

The great portent that appeared in heaven is inseparable from the woman's Son who is himself heaven. The heavenly city described in the Book of Revelation (21:12) has twelve gates, because the ways into it are numerous. But Mary is pre-eminently 'the gate of heaven that is always open'. The lowly handmaid of the Lord and of men and women, she is the gate and the gate-keeper. Through her the Son came into the world, to her the beloved disciple was entrusted, as to the entire Church, so that she might lead him into heaven.

* * *

In numerous religious houses the community gathers for a final prayer as night falls before the candle-lit statue or icon of the mother of Christ. The prayer opens with a greeting: 'Hail, holy queen...' It concludes with a request: 'And after this our exile show unto us the blessed fruit of thy womb, Jesus.'

We have greeted Mary in her grace of motherhood, icon of the Spirit; we have contemplated the icon of the Church, Mary at the heart of the history of salvation. At the moment when we complete our meditation before her holy image our look becomes one of supplication: 'Show unto us the blessed fruit of thy womb, Jesus.' It is 'to find the child with Mary, his mother' (cf Mt 2:11) that 'the disciple took her to his own home' (Jn 19:27).

She would not be able to remain deaf to this prayer, for in her dwells the Holy Spirit of whom Jesus said: 'He will guide you into all the truth' (Jn 16:13).

34. St Peter Damian, Opusc. XI: *Dominus vobiscum* 5 and 6, PL 145:235.

35. The application of the term 'Church' to Israel is not an anachronism. It is a translation of the Hebrew word *qahal* which denotes the assembly of Israel and which in Greek is translated as *ecclesia*, assembly – the word which came to mean 'Church' and from which the Romance and Celtic languages derive their word for 'Church'.

36. St Augustine, *De civitate Dei* 17:11, CCL 48:575.

37. Quodvultdeus, *De symbolo ad catechumenos* 3:1, CCL 60:349.

38. Tertullian, *De resurrectione mortuorum* 8:2, CCL 2:931: '*Ideo caro salutis est cardo.*'

39. Cf St Ambrose, *In Ps. 118 Sermo 1:16,* CSEL 62:16.

40. It is in this way that, from John 1:29-33, Jesus is proclaimed as the heavenly lamb on whom the Spirit rests, who baptizes in the Spirit and thus takes away the sin of the world (Jn 19:30,34; cf Jn 7:37-39), in the holiness of the Spirit (Jn 20:22-33).

41. Perhaps we ought to translate: 'Has not my hour come yet?', the final hour that has already been anticipated in the miracle at Cana.

42. For John 'the truth' designates the full enlightened reality, in contrast to transitory earthly realities that lack eternity.

43. Paul Claudel, *Stabat Mater, 8 février 1944. Revue des Deux Mondes, 15 avril 1944.* Ed. de La Pléiade, *Œuvres poétiques*, p. 590.

44. Glory does not empty out Jesus' death: rather it maintains Jesus for ever in his death, that is to say at the culmination of his earthly life, at the summit of his ascent to the Father, in the fullness of obedience and his redemptive merit. Jesus is glorified in what his glory achieves, that is to say in his death. The cross is the eternal throne of his royalty (Jn 13:32-33, Rev 5:6).

45. Protestant thinking objects to the idea of the Church,

and thus Mary, sharing in the work of salvation. It believes it has to reject this in the name of Christ's unique mediation: 'There is one mediator between God and men' (1 Tim 2:5).

In the theology dear to the Reformers, Christ pays an infinite price for us and thus makes satisfaction to God's justice that has been offended. It is logical to conclude from this that Christ's mediation is exclusive of all other participation, he alone being in a position to pay such a price. What falls to men and women is to believe that Christ has paid this price, that justice has been 'satisfied', and to receive passively, each on his or her own account, the pardon that in this way has been merited by Christ.

Scripture offers us a different picture of the works of salvation which cannot be reduced to paying a debt. The admittedly scriptural image of the ransom that has been paid is very badly interpreted in this theology (cf my work *Le Père, Dieu en son mystère*, Paris 1967, pp. 57-62). Jesus has not only obtained for us the right to forgiveness but in his passover he has become the mystery of salvation: 'He has become for us... redemption' (1 Cor 1:30 translated literally). Man benefits from redemption not by the application of merits but by communion with Christ who, in his death and resurrection, is our salvation. The eucharist illustrates this: in it the body of Christ is given to the Church in his death and resurrection so that the Church may become a single body with him in this mystery which is the salvation of the world. The Church is saved in this participation, at one and the same time saved and saving through communion, in complete subordination to the one and only act of redemption. The one and only mediator includes and embodies men and women in his mystery: the one and only mediation is that of the 'true vine' (Jn 15:1-8) where the rootstock, the source of life, bears fruit together with the shoots.

46. Cf for example the Letter of the Christians of Lyons and Vienne quoted by Eusebius of Caesarea, *Historia ecclesiastica* V:1:45.

47. J. J. Olier, *Vie intérieure de la très sainte Vierge*, Paris, 1875, pp. 241-242. The French school of spirituality had the intuition of a theology of the paschal mystery at a

time when the generality of theologians had for centuries drawn their inspiration from juridical categories and ignored the salvific meaning of Jesus' resurrection. It also discovered in Mary 'the Church enclosed and epitomized'. I hope I may be allowed a personal observation. Having long ago, round about the 1940's, studied the redemption as paschal mystery, I understood from then on that Mary represents the entire Church. Vatican II honoured at one and the same time the theology of the paschal mystery and that of Mary, the Church's countenance. Once one has grasped the redemption as paschal mystery one realizes that the mystery of the Church finds its image in Mary. To overcome the obstacle of Mary in dialogue with Protestantism it would perhaps be enough if the partners were firmly to disengage themselves from juridical categories in their theology and consider redemption as paschal mystery.

48. Cf F. X. Durrwell, *L'Esprit Saint de Dieu*, Paris, 1983, pp. 90-97: English translation, *Holy Spirit of God*, London, 1986.

49. St Thomas Aquinas, *Summa Theologiae* II II 1. 17 art. 3.

50. Cf F. X. Durrwell, *L'Esprit Saint de Dieu*, Paris, 1983, pp. 138-146: English translation, *Holy Spirit of God* , London, 1986.

51. Paul Claudel, *La Vierge á midi*.

52. See I. de la Potterie, *Marie dans le mystère de l'alliance*, Paris, 1987, p. 249. The verb 'take' used by the evangelist strengthens the idea of welcoming when it is a person that is involved (cf Jn 1:11-12). The phrase translated 'to his own home' does not refer only to things that are material, spatial. It is used in John 1:11: 'He came to his own home and his own people received him not.'

53. Cf Rudolf Schnackenburg, *The gospel according to John*, vol. 3, London and Tunbridge Wells, 1982, pp. 284-285.

54. *Servus Mariae nunquam peribit.* This conviction has been expressed throughout the centuries of Christian history. Two popes of modern times have lent their authority to confirm it: 'Among Christians the consistently held opinion, confirmed by long experience, is that those who have recourse to this same Virgin as

their patron shall not perish eternally', Benedict XV, *Inter sodalicia*, AAS 10 (1918), p. 182. 'We know full well that everywhere that the most blessed Mother of God is venerated with sincere and zealous devotion the hope of salvation can never be lacking', Pius XII, *Sacro vergente anno*, AAS 44 (1952), p. 510.

55. It is worth asking whether on earth a human being can commit a sin that cuts him or her off radically from the source of grace. Would not someone committing such a sin be already in hell? One can pray for every man and woman on earth with the hope of saving them.

56. The RSV translates 1 John 5:16: 'he will ask and God will give him life.' According to this translation, the Church's mediation consists of praying to God, but not of giving life. However (as a footnote in the RSV indicates) the Greek text says: 'he will ask, and he will give him life.' The RSV translation would be justified if the text had read 'and life will be given him', since in the Bible the passive is often used to denote an action for which God is responsible. Here, the person who prays shares in the giving of life, which nevertheless comes from God. A good commentary on this passage is provided by the Church of Lyons, thoroughly permeated with Johannine thinking, in its Letter describing the persecution it endured in 177 A.D. Several Christians had fallen away, not daring to profess their faith before the judge. But the others 'from their own abundance supplied with a mother's love those that needed, and shedding many tears for them to the Father, they prayed for life and he gave it to them, and they divided it among their neighbours' (Eusebius of Caesarea, *Historia ecclesiastica* V:2:6).

57. The beginnings of six strophes of a poem by Didier Rimaud used in the Office of the Assumption in the French liturgy.

58. I hope I may be allowed yet another reference to my book *L'Esprit Saint de Dieu*, Paris, 1983, pp. 171-173.

59. Paul Verlaine, *Sagesse*, Éd. de la Pléiade, 1965, p. 266.

60. Charles Péguy, *Le mystère des saints Innocents*, NRF Gallimard, p. 179.

61. Paul Claudel, *La Vierge à midi*.

62. Among other testimonies worth citing is that of Pierre Emmanuel: 'Prayer to Mary persisted even at times when I had no actual link with the Church.' Cf *Informations catholiques internationales*, 2 mai 1974, p. 17.

63. *Alma Redemptoris mater, quae pervia caeli porta manes...*

THE SONG OF SALVATION

Isidro Gomà Civit

The present study is an invitation to a living understanding of the Song of Mary and its place in the heart of the Church. It is the distillation of many lectures in exegesis, given at various times to various groups. In it Mgr Gomà achieves a rare and happy combination of authentic scholarship and true, deep, spirituality. His aim is for his readers to penetrate ever more deeply into the *Magnificat*, using every means available to increase not only their understanding of its import and background but their own ability to enter into its spirit and make it more completely their own.

Ample notes and bibliography provide openings for those who would wish to go even more deeply into certain aspects of the Song of Mary. Those who are not so much interested in exact scholarship will nevertheless find much to satisfy them in these pages, which are intended as much, or more, to deepen the reader's spiritual life as to widen his/her knowledge. This is no dry, scholastic study, though its scholarship is beyond reproach, but is all alive with the love and enthusiasm of one who longs to share his own ability to make this prayer, bequeathed to the Church by its earliest members, truly one's own.

159 pages   ISBN 085439 260 2   £5.95

MARY FOR TODAY

Hans-Urs von Balthasar

What does Mary mean for today's men and women? That is the question Hans-Urs von Balthasar sets out to answer. Dogmatism in language and one-sidedness in Marian cult have, in many ways, shifted attention from the fulness and deepness of the Marian mystery. The distinguished Swiss theologian shows here new possibilities to meet Mary in a more authentic way. With a masterly combination of theological consideration and spiritual mediation, he explores what the New Testament tells us about the mother of God and places Mary in the Horizon of our time, portraying her as icon – a model of convincing praxis of faith: Mary mother of believers: Mary, the Church in origin.

72 pages   ISBN 085439 2661   £2.50

REJOICE MARY

Giancarlo Bruni

Among the praises handed down to us through the centuries none equals the Hail Mary in its eminently scriptural content and character.

This book is an earnest attempt to capture the biblical resonances of the Hail Mary following the method of the *Lectio Divina*, a meditative and prayerful way of studying the Scriptures under the guidance of the Holy Spirit and in the company of the saints.

Thus in *Rejoice Mary* the reader is led to rediscover anew the crystalline beauty and simplicity of the Hail Mary disclosed by the radiance of the Divine Word.

94 pages   ISBN 085439 278 5   £3.25